ANGLICAN ORDERS

ANGLICAN ORDERS

by

ANTHONY A. STEPHENSON, S.J.

With Appendices by

WALTON HANNAH
and
HUGH ROSS WILLIAMSON

THE NEWMAN PRESS
WESTMINSTER, MARYLAND

DE LICENTIA SVPERIORVM ORDINIS

NIHIL OBSTAT: JOHANNES M. T. BARTON, S.T.D., L.S.S.
CENSOR DEPVTATVS
IMPRIMATVR: E. MORROGH BERNARD
VICARIVS GENERALIS
WESTMONASTERII: DIE XX FEBRVARII MCMLVI

First published 1956
PRINTED IN GREAT BRITAIN

CONTENTS

	Page
PREFACE	7

Part I

1 THE THEOLOGY 15
2 THE ARGUMENT OF GREGORY DIX 23
3 THE ORDINAL OF 1552 32

Part II

4 DR. MASCALL ON ORDINATION 40
5 THE HUNTING OF THE HOBBIT: A Reply by Dr. E. L. Mascall 50
6 IN FULL CRY: A Rejoinder to Dr. Mascall 58

Appendices

I MINISTERIAL INTENTION 66
II THE TEXT OF *Apostolicae Curae*, CHAP. 33 69
III A LETTER FROM WALTON HANNAH 70
IV A CONVERT EXPLAINS, BY HUGH ROSS WILLIAMSON 74

Preface

IT MUST BE CONFESSED that the title of this book is not quite accurate, since the book is concerned directly only with priestly Orders. However, since the episcopate is the *Summum Sacerdotium*, or High Priesthood, some of the following pages have a general relevance to the conditions of a valid rite for consecrating bishops also.

A reader of my five articles on Anglican Orders in *The Month*, reprinted here without substantial change, remarked that the whole argument turns on a rather fine point. In the main this remark seems to me untrue, since the objection to the Catholic validity of Anglican Orders is simply the old and plain objection that the sixteenth-century English Reformers rejected the Mass and, with it, Catholic Orders.

It is, however, true that in order to refute some ingenious Anglican defences it is necessary, in exposing the fallacies in these arguments, to draw certain distinctions and to reason in a way that makes some demands on the attention of the reader. A position arises rather like that in certain legal cases. The governing facts of the case may be plain enough; yet if brilliant barristers (it may be in all sincerity) plead the false cause with persuasive eloquence, then, to prevent the jury being misled in the *cause célèbre* which may ensue, the opposing counsel and the judge may be driven to some rather subtle exposition in identifying and characterising the principal relevant facts and in explaining the nature and application of the governing principles. This analogy is not altogether fanciful. For it so happens that that distinguished scholar, the late Dom Gregory Dix, whose book *The Question of Anglican Orders* was so influential in sustaining and rationalising Anglican opinion, frankly admitted no less than three times in the course of that work (be it said to his credit) that he wrote, not with the objectivity and impartiality of a judge, but as an advocate presenting a case, though a case in which he believed. For my part I can say in all honesty that I have approached and studied this problem dispassionately, ready to follow where the argument led. By temperament, indeed, a bridge-builder rather than a controversialist, had I allowed myself to be swayed by emotion or inclination, I should have been prejudiced in favour of a solution offering hopes of a corporate or group reconciliation of Anglo-Catholics to the Holy See. When, therefore, towards the beginning of last year—at that time some elements in the problem still perplexed me—some Anglican Papalist friends lent me Gregory Dix's *The Question of Anglican Orders* and C. F. Hrauda's *Anglican Ordinations*, together with the late Victor Roberts's *In Terra Aliena*, I was prepared to find new arguments in these works. The more closely, however, one studied the question, the clearer it became that these writers altogether failed to prove their case; their advocacy was as unconvincing as the Anglican Archbishops' *Reply* of 1897.

If this conclusion must fail to encourage Anglo-Catholic ecumenist aspirations, yet at least the Anglican Papalists—assuming they are convinced by it—should welcome this book; I pray that it may remove the one conscientious difficulty that stands between them and the Catholic Church. In any case, this book has been prompted by the belief that, after charity, clarity can contribute most to the cause of Christian unity. Something decisive happened at the English Reformation, and no good, but only grievous harm, can come from blinding oneself to this fact.

Perhaps I may be allowed at this point, for the benefit of the general reader or the newcomer to this controversy, to explain briefly what are the determining documents in the dispute. In pre-Reformation England Ordinations were performed by the rites contained in the Sarum Pontifical; this Catholic Pontifical is sometimes referred to simply as "the Pontifical"; it is substantially the same as the Pontifical in use in the Western Catholic Church today. In 1550 the English Reformers replaced the rite of the Pontifical by that of a new Ordinal. Two years later the Reformers revised their new Ordinal in a more decidedly Protestant direction, and, after the brief interruption of Mary's reign, this revised new Ordinal of 1552 was in constant use in the Anglican, or English Reformed, Church from the accession of Queen Elizabeth in 1559 until 1662. It is this Ordinal of 1552, therefore, that is of vital importance; it is here sometimes referred to simply as "the Ordinal." It is obvious that if the Ordinal of 1552 lacked Catholic validity (and its character can best be judged by comparing its rites with those of the Catholic Pontifical for which it was substituted), then by 1662 the Apostolic succession and all true Orders had been lost, and no changes made in that year could in themselves retrieve the situation.

In the Catholic Pontifical the Preface of the Ordination Mass sung by the bishop contains the consecratory prayer and the actual "form" of the sacrament of priestly Ordination. The "Preface," however, which plays so prominent a part in the controversy is not this Mass Preface, but the preface (foreword) to the Reformers' Ordinal of 1552. This Preface is no part of the Ordination rite (it is not prescribed to be read before Ordinations), still less of the essential part of the rite, the sacramental "form." Nevertheless, if the internal evidence—the text of the 1552 rite itself—were not decisive, the Preface, had it declared a clear and explicit Catholic doctrine of the priesthood, could have been external evidence of the first importance, giving a Catholic character to an ambiguous or neutral form. In fact the case is just the reverse. The Ordinal of 1552 is decisively and unambiguously heretical: its form is a mutilation of the Catholic form, from which every vestige of the Catholic conception of the sacrificing priesthood has been stripped. The Preface, on the other hand, is vague and ambiguous; on the crucial question of the nature of the ministry and the Eucharist it is silent.

For the sake of completeness it may be mentioned here that the Ordinal prescribed that the ceremony for the Ordering of Priests should be introduced by a sermon "declaring the Duty and Office of such as come to be admitted Priests; how necessary that Order is in the Church of Christ." But here, again, no guidance is given to the preacher in his task of defining the duties of the priests made by the new Ordinal. No one denies that the English Reformers regarded the priesthood as a necessary qualification for celebrating the Lord's Supper; the question is whether the service of the Lord's Supper was regarded as anything more than a commemorative ritual feast.

The "Black Rubric" first appeared in the Communion service of the second Prayer Book. Omitted in the 1559 edition, it was reintroduced in 1662 with the change of "real or essential presence" to "corporal presence." It explains clearly that, although the Prayer Book prescribes that communicants should communicate kneeling, "yet, lest the same kneeling should by any persons, either out of ignorance and infirmity, or out of malice and obstinacy, be misconstrued and depraved; It is hereby declared,

That thereby no adoration is intended, or ought to be done, either unto the Sacramental Bread or Wine there bodily received, or unto any Corporal Presence of Christ's natural Flesh and Blood." One would have thought that this was plain enough. Yet Anglo-Catholics have argued that what was excluded was only crude and superstitious theories of the Real Presence, not the Real Presence itself. This argument appears, in principle, to offer some sort of escape from almost all possible difficulties. They argue also that it is natural to describe Christ's Eucharistic presence, though true and real, as "spiritual" rather than "corporal." But it must surely be admitted that this Rubric is a direct denial of the traditional Catholic belief that in the Sacrament Christ *is* present "corporally"—present body and blood, soul and divinity, true Man and true God. Is it not clear that all that the Rubric is prepared to allow is that sort of spiritual presence (even if in a privileged degree) which is promised wherever two or three are gathered in Christ's name? It is natural enough that on this theory kneeling should be prescribed, if only "for a signification of our grateful and humble acknowledgement of the benefits of Christ therein given ... and for the avoiding of such profanation and disorder in the holy Communion as might otherwise ensue";[1] but it then, of course, becomes necessary to explain that kneeling does not imply a belief in the Catholic doctrine of a real and objective presence of Christ. Suppose, on the other hand, a church which prescribes kneeling at Communion because it holds the Catholic belief that in the Eucharist Christ is present as really, though sacramentally, as He was at Emmaus or in the Supper Room in Jerusalem; suppose this church concerned because of the growth among its members of some "crude" interpretation of the Real Presence (whatever this "crude" interpretation could be): can one imagine this church formally explaining in a rubric in its liturgy that this crude theory is not implied by the custom of kneeling? The notion is surely ludicrous. Is there any conceivable reason why any sane person should be tempted to *suppose* that the practice of kneeling implied the crude variation rather than the authentic Catholic doctrine? The Black Rubric makes sense only on the supposition that the Eucharistic doctrine of the Church which placed it in its liturgy did not obviously and

---

[1] The quotation is from the "Black Rubric."

automatically imply a kneeling posture for the communicant.[1]

To arrive at a decision on the question of the validity of Anglican Orders, it is essential that the whole argument and all the relevant facts be considered together. Yet the main outline of the argument can be briefly sketched. The most important distinction to be drawn need present no difficulty: the distinction between the subjective intention of the minister in conferring a sacrament and the meaning of the "form" of the sacrament.[2] The fundamental defect in the Ordinal of 1552 is a defect of form, a defect, that is, in those words of the rite which express the power that is being bestowed. As in an analogous legal case where someone, let us say, changed the traditional form for conferring some legal power or for conferring a commission in Her Majesty's armed forces, in determining the validity of the new form everything turns on its *meaning*—does it express essentially the same thing as the old form? If the form were in itself ambiguous or neutral, and so insufficient or doubtful, it could, indeed, be saved if the party framing it issued an accompanying declaration, interpreting and explicitly specifying the meaning of the form in the correct or orthodox sense. If, however, the person or body changing the form owing to doubt or ignorance concerning the real nature of the power to be conveyed, has simply the general, unspecified, or

---

[1] It is, of course, clear beyond the possibility of denial that the "Black Rubric," like the Twenty-eighth of the XXXIX Articles, denies Transubstantiation. It is, however, logically possible to deny Transubstantiation but to accept the doctrine of the Real Presence, since it is logically possible for Christ to be made present by the Words of Institution without the bread and wine being changed into His Body and Blood. But, apart from the arguments adduced in the text, since the traditional Catholic belief was that the Real Presence is effected by the transubstantiation of the elements, and considering further that at the time of the Reformation there was a widespread rejection of both beliefs together, the denial of Transubstantiation, unless accompanied by a firm disclaimer of the other denial (of the denial, that is, of the Real Presence), which simple people would naturally suppose to be a consequence of the first, creates a presumption that the Real Presence was also denied.

[2] In Catholic theology the meaning of the form is called the objective intention. It is similar to what Anglican theologians commonly mean by the word "intention" when unqualified; in Anglican usage, however, "intention" does not appear to be altogether the same thing as the "objective sense" of the form; it is rather more subjective, something that can be "put upon" the form from the outside by the officially expressed doctrine of the church using the form. This is a legitimate conception; but it is important to recognise that its application is limited; only within definite limits can an "intention" be "put upon" a sacramental form. If the objective meaning of the form is already sufficiently determinate and clear in itself, a quite alien "intention" cannot arbitrarily be placed upon it.

"blind"[1] intention of doing the right thing (in our case, of "doing what Christ instituted, whatever that may be"), this will be of no avail if the new form has been fatally changed. For the new form no longer expresses the old thing, and a general pious intention, however laudable, will not correct its *meaning*.

The core of the case against Anglican Orders is plain enough. Because they rejected Catholic Eucharistic doctrine, the English Reformers mutilated the Catholic Ordination rite, eliminating from it all prayers, phrases and ceremonies referring to the Mass and the sacrificing Christian priesthood.

Anglo-Catholics argue that the Ordinal was saved by its Preface. The Preface, after observing that "from the Apostles' time there have been these Orders of Ministers in Christ's Church; Bishops, Priests, and Deacons," states the intention of "continuing" these Orders. In determining what, if any, bearing the Preface has on the essential point—the meaning of the Ordination rite of 1552—it is necessary to take into account many considerations, of which I here select six.

(1) If the sacramental form has itself a clearly heretical meaning, no external evidence (such as is the Preface) can be admitted. And the plain fact is that the action of the Reformers in so mutilating the Catholic Pontifical as to remove from it, at point after point, every trace of, or reference to, the Christian Sacrifice and the priest's power over the (physical) Body of Christ, is final and decisive.

(2) Nevertheless, if, almost *per impossibile*, the Preface had openly professed the traditional doctrine of the Mass and had stated its intention to ordain Catholic priests in the traditional sense, a pretty theological problem would have arisen. In fact, however, nothing approaching such a statement is to be found in the Preface, which nowhere asserts that the Catholic thing—or anything more than the *name* of the priesthood—is to be continued. Moreover the evidence, at best equivocal, of the Preface is outweighed by other external evidence: for example, by the much clearer evidence of the XXXIX Articles and the unambiguously

---

[1] By a "blind" intention I mean the sort of intention an uninstructed Mohammedan might have in giving Christian Baptism, such an intention as he might formulate to himself thus: "I intend to operate on the sacramental plane, *or* to perform this ritual act for what it is worth, *or* to do what the Christians believe they do by this act—whatever that may be." This is sufficient *if* he keeps the right matter and form.

clear evidence of the main stream of English reformed theology in the sixteenth century.

(3) The doctrine of these theologians—some striking passages are quoted in Chapter 2—shows quite plainly that the character of the mutilation of the Catholic rite (the deletion of ceremonies and phrases referring to the Mass) was no accident, but deliberately intended. It also shows that the rejection, in the Thirty-first of the XXXIX Articles, of "the Sacrifices of Masses" was a rejection, not of false or superstitious theories of the Mass, but of the Mass itself.

(4) When one remembers how for centuries English Protestants mocked and outlawed the Mass and the Catholic priesthood—until comparatively recent times the Anglican parson was contrasted, in the public mind, with the Catholic "Massing" priest in virtue of his *function*—it would be an astonishing paradox if during all that time, indeed ever since 1552, the English Protestant Church had itself been not only making sacrificing priests, indistinguishable from Catholic priests in respect of their office, but had actually been *meaning* to do so. And yet the whole modern Anglican contention that the Church of England has Catholic Orders depends on the position that this *was* the meaning and intention of the Ordinal of 1552. The late C. F. Hrauda touched on an allied anomaly when he remarked, supposing the ministers ordained by the Ordinal to have been true priests, that they would have effected the sacrament, transubstantiated the elements and celebrated Mass when they pronounced the words of consecration, even though they never suspected that they were doing so. This is perfectly true; for on the supposition that they were priests, they would have been valid ministers using the correct form and (presumably) having the intention of doing what Christ instituted. But Hrauda overlooked the real, the impossible, paradox, as well as the fallacy underlying his assumption that the Ordinal's ministers were true priests. He failed to advert sufficiently to the consequences of the fact that in the *other* sacrament, the sacrament of Orders itself, the Reformers' error about the Eucharist, and consequently about the power to be bestowed in Ordination, had led them to change and invalidate the *form*. His frank admission (from which the hypothetical paradox he discusses arises) that the Ordinal's priests did not believe that they were saying Mass, is a direct denial of the contention which is a main prop of the Anglo-

Catholic position: the contention, that is, that the Ordinal, in virtue of its Preface, did *intend* to make sacrificing priests.

(5) The important principle stated early in Chapter 3.

(6) The judgement, even today, not only of the "Protestant" wing of the Church of England, but also of such eminent Anglican scholars as the Dixie Professor of Ecclesiastic History in Cambridge and Professor H. A. Hodges on the true character of Anglicanism. Last year Professor Hodges insisted (*Anglicanism and Orthodoxy*) that the Articles, the Ordinal, the Prayer Book and the Catechism are all predominantly Protestant; and this year has seen Professor Norman Sykes's scholarly demonstration that the authentic Anglican tradition has never regarded bishops as essential to the Church of Christ or deemed non-episcopal ministries invalid.

At Dr. Eric Mascall's request, I point out that his single chapter (to which the Imprimatur, incidentally, does not apply) is not intended to be an answer to every point raised in my first four chapters, and that the questions at issue between us are primarily theological rather than historical—"differences about the nature of the Church, the sacraments and the ministry." The clue I should give to my own final chapter is this: Dr. Mascall's theory makes Ordination comparable, in its mode, to election or co-option to a club or other corporation, so that, provided the club is identified, the powers conferred need not be indicated at all. There is no reason to believe this theory to be true; and, if it were true, Anglican Orders would be more obviously invalid than ever—though for a quite different reason—schism. For, on this theory, considerations of will, authority and constitutional legitimacy become paramount.

My thanks are due to Fr. Philip Caraman, S.J., Editor of *The Month*, in whose pages (July, August, September, November, December 1955 and February 1956) the substance of this book first appeared, for permission to reprint my articles here. I am similarly indebted to the distinguished authors of Chapter 5 and Appendices III and IV respectively. I gladly acknowledge my indebtedness to the valuable aid of Fr. W. Dempsey, S.J., at various points and of Fr. J. H. Crehan, S.J., in my discussion of the Serapion rite.

A. A. STEPHENSON, S.J.

114 Mount Street, London, W.1.   *29th February*, 1956.

PART I

1

The Theology

THE RECENT STORM in the Church of England over the recognition of the new presbyters in the Church of South India makes this an opportune moment for a concise and impartial discussion of the controversial question of the validity of Anglican Orders. Indeed for most "Anglican Papalists," as well as for the closely related group for whom some years ago the late Victor Roberts spoke in *In Terra Aliena*,[1] the question of the validity of their Orders is crucial, and belief in this validity is the sole barrier to their reconciliation to the Church from which they are regretfully in exile. In two striking sentences *In Terra Aliena* summed up the position of the group whose views it voiced:

> We who belong to this minority admit that we are in schism, though not by our own fault, and we desire nothing more ardently than to be in visible communion with the Holy See. Our only reason for remaining in schism is that we cannot rid ourselves of the belief that the validity of Anglican Orders is a matter of *truth*, and therefore we cannot accept reconciliation with Rome at the price of denying in word or action what we believe to be true.[2]

For them, belief in the validity of their Orders grounds a conscientious objection to submission to the Church on terms of re-Ordination if they wish to go forward to the priesthood.

These Anglican Papalists differ from the Anglo-Catholics in not holding that possession of valid Orders justifies the existence

---

[1] *In Terra Aliena* gives a valuable and moving account of the difficulties—largely psychological or practical, and by no means insuperable—which the Anglican Papalist encounters in his path to Rome. Printed for private circulation (no date, no price), it is sub-titled "An *Apologia* for those who accept the authority of the Holy See, yet, being unable to repudiate the validity of Anglican orders, remain outside the Roman Unity."

[2] P. 1.

of the Church of England. Anglo-Catholics claim that it does, although one would have thought that only fundamentally different convictions about doctrine or Church order could even subjectively justify what they must regard as the rending of at least the visible Catholic unity. In any case their view of the Church of England as a branch of the Catholic Church likewise depends on the truth of their claim to possess valid Orders. The Low Church and "Protestant" groups of Anglican clergy presumably have little interest in the question, as they would be shocked by the thought that they say Mass or are priests in the traditional Catholic sense.

Since even those Anglicans who admit Papal infallibility hold that Pope Leo XIII's Apostolical Letter, *Apostolicae curae*, is not infallible and assert that its decision is incompatible with Catholic theological principles, the most useful course will be to discuss the question on its merits in the light of Catholic theology.

Since a sacramental rite causes, *ex opere operato*, the effect which it signifies, all that is required for validity is that a properly qualified minister shall, having the intention of effecting a Christian sacrament, apply the correct matter and form to an apt subject.

The minister of Holy Orders must be a bishop. He is disqualified, so far as validity goes, neither by heresy nor schism (material or formal) nor even by apostasy.

In speaking of the necessary intention, a distinction is sometimes drawn between subjective intention (the intention of the minister) and objective intention, which is virtually the same thing as the meaning of the form.[1] To avoid ambiguity, "intention" will regularly be used here to denote the subjective intention of the minister.

Per se, or in the absence of complications, very little is required on the score of intention. Theologians generally discuss the subject with two types of situation in mind. What sort of intention is required in a priest when consecrating at Mass or baptising? Full attention is not necessary; distractions do not invalidate the sacrament. It is sufficient that the minister have at least a virtual intention of "doing what the Church does," or of effecting a Christian sacrament. The other type of case commonly discussed is that of a heretic or infidel conferring a sacrament. The classical

[1] See Preface, p. 11, n. 2.

case so often cited by the theologians, that of a Mohammedan consenting to baptise the baby of a Christian woman dying in the desert, illustrates the relevant points. It is sufficient that the Moslem intend (at least implicitly by virtue of his consent) to confer a Christian sacrament: to baptise the baby, not just bath it. The sufficiency of this intention would not be affected by the fact that the Saracen privately regarded the whole proceedings as nonsense and was only indulging a dying woman's whim. But in the theologians' discussions of all such cases, be it noted, it is always presupposed that the proper rite has been used, that the matter and form have been correct.

Erroneous beliefs, therefore, are not in themselves incompatible with a sufficient intention. But along with his general intention of conferring a Christian sacrament a heretical minister may have a second, specific, intention which contradicts and nullifies the first. If, for instance, a bishop holding Pneumatomachian views should intend to confirm, but at the same time should obstinately intend not to bestow the Holy Ghost, then validity would be doubtful. When there are two contrary intentions, validity probably depends on which is the overriding intention. When the form is kept, intention is generally presumed.

There are strong reasons for thinking that the English reformed bishops in the sixteenth century were so hostile to the Mass and the Catholic conception of the priesthood that their deliberate intention (manifested in the very changes they made in the rite) of excluding the power of sacrifice, nullified any general intention they may have had of conferring a Christian sacrament. It is, indeed, very doubtful if the Reformers even understood that Ordination was a sacrament. The 25th of the XXXIX Articles (where Gregory Dix bade us look for authentic Anglican doctrine) clearly states that there are only two sacraments, Baptism and the Lord's Supper. These two, the Article states, are the only two instituted by Christ (institution by Christ is an essential element in a sacrament). The Article is explicit that Order is not to be counted for a sacrament of the Gospel. One is left to choose between the alternative views that it is an institution "sprung of the corrupt following of the Apostles," or that it is one of those "states of life allowed in the Scriptures" but not consecrated by "any visible sign or ceremony ordained of God."

It is probable, therefore, that Anglican Orders would be

invalid on grounds of defect of intention alone, even had heretical intention and belief not led to the mutilation, in essentials, of the Catholic form. It is, however, defect of form (to be discussed presently) that is decisive. For it is hard to claim certainty for the argument from intention alone (while supposing, for argument's sake, the validity of the form), since this would involve knowing both that particular persons at a particular moment (the moment of performing the sacrament) deliberately intended not to make sacrificing priests, and that this intention prevailed over a possible intention of conferring a Christian sacrament. Normally, therefore, when the correct rite has been followed sufficient intention is presumed; but once it is proved that matter or form was deliberately mutilated in essentials, then the presumption is that there was defect of intention also. As the great Leo said: "With this defect of form, therefore, is combined a defect of intention.... Concerning the mind or intention in itself, which is something internal, the Church does not pass judgment; but she is bound to judge of it so far as it is externally manifested."[1]

The primary and quite decisive argument, therefore, against the validity of Anglican Orders is that from substantial defect in the form of the rite in the second Edwardian Ordinal (1552). Priestly Ordination confers the power and grace of the priesthood, an essential part of which is the power to act as Christ's minister at the altar, to change the bread into the Body of Christ and the wine into His Blood, and to offer the Victim of Calvary. The principles relating to the sacramental rite are few and clear. A sacrament is a sign which produces the grace which it signifies, and it must signify the grace which it effects. Generally the signification of the sacramental matter is relatively indeterminate and vague; it is further determined, *i.e.*, given sufficient precision, by the form. Thus in the Ordination of a priest the matter is the first imposition of hands by the bishop; but since this, which is also the matter in Confirmation, by no means unambiguously signifies the bestowal of the grace and power of the priesthood, it is complemented by the words of the form: "Bestow, almighty God, upon this Thy servant the dignity of the Priesthood . . ."[2] In judging the validity of the form, every-

[1] *Apostolicae curae*, Canon G. D. Smith's trans., n. 33, in C.T.S. pamphlet H. 311.
[2] Cf. the Apostolic Constitution, *De Sacris Ordinibus*, given by Pope Pius XII, 30 Nov. 1947; *A.A.S.*, 40 (1948), pp. 5–7.

thing depends on the *meaning* of the words used. If the form is changed, the sacrament is invalid if the change is essential; otherwise it is valid. Exact verbal adherence to the approved form is not necessary for validity; synonymous words suffice. Thus if a priest, forgetting the words of absolution, were to say instead, "As the representative of Christ, I forgive you your sins," the sacrament would be valid. On the other hand, the change or omission of anything essential invalidates the sacrament. Thus Vermeersch judges the following forms insufficient for Baptism: "I baptise you in the name of the Blessed Trinity," or "I baptise you in the name of the Father and of the Son," or even (as implicitly denying the Monarchy, or substantial unity of God) "I baptise you in the name*s* of the Father and of the Son and of the Holy Ghost."[1]

As the minister's erroneous or heretical beliefs do not of themselves invalidate a sacrament, so neither can an orthodox intention heal an essentially defective or positively erroneous form. Intention and beliefs can be relevant to the validity of a form by affecting its *meaning*, but only so. Anglican controversialists are mistaken when they suggest that the validity of the ancient Catholic rite of Serapion was directly secured by the orthodox intention of the ministers in spite of a defective form. The Serapion rite was discovered (in an incomplete text in a single manuscript) very soon after the appearance of *Apostolicae curae* in 1896 and was at the time regarded by Anglicans as an answer to prayer. Indeed, only ten years ago Dix was making considerable controversial play with it. But further study has shown that the difficulty is only apparent, a matter of understanding Serapion's idiom; once that is understood, it becomes clear that the Serapion Ordination rite sufficiently signified, in the terminology of the fourth-century Egyptian Church, the bestowal of the true grace and power of the priesthood.

Anglicans, therefore, have been unreasonable when they have complained that Pope Leo, in his condemnation of Anglican Orders, did not expressly refer to the statement of intention in the Preface to the Edwardian Ordinal. For the Preface could be relevant to the problem only in three ways. It might be evidence of the general intention of conferring a Christian sacrament: but that cannot avail against the decisive evidence of a specific

[1] A. Vermeersch, S.J., *Theologiae Moralis, etc.*, t. III (1927), 190.

intention (manifested in the very mutilation of the form) that was anti-Catholic and incompatible with the nature of the sacrament. The Preface might also be invoked as evidence concerning the *specific* intention of the minister, or of the English Church, or concerning the meaning of the form. But from both these points of view the Preface is only a fraction of the total evidence available and, owing to its studied vagueness, is of much less value than the clear evidence derivable from the mutilation of the Catholic form, as well as from the XXXIX Articles, the Protestant theology of Cranmer, and the special variety of English reformed theology which, with such disastrous results, triumphed in the decisive years.

Beliefs can indirectly affect the meaning of a sacramental rite, and so the validity of the sacrament, by affecting language: for example, if, in consequence of a theological revolution, the word "priest" in a particular historical and liturgical context bears a meaning utterly different from the traditional Christian meaning. In Hooker's *Laws of Ecclesiastical Polity* there is an excellent example of what the word meant not only to the best known of the Elizabethan Anglican divines, but also, apparently, to the general body of the Anglican laity in 1585.

> Seeing then that sacrifice is now no part of the Church ministry, how should the name of Priesthood be thereunto rightly applied? Surely even as St. Paul applieth the name of flesh unto that very substance of fishes, which hath a proportionable correspondence to flesh, although it be in nature another thing. Whereupon, when philosophers will speak warily, they make a difference between flesh in one sort of living creatures, and that other substance in the rest which hath but a kind of analogy to flesh. ... The Fathers of the Church of Christ with like security of speech, call usually the ministry of the Gospel *Priesthood*, in regard of that which the Gospel hath proportionable to ancient sacrifices; namely, the Communion of the blessed Body and Blood of Christ, *although it hath properly now no sacrifice*. As for the people, when they hear the name, it draweth no more their minds to any cogitation of sacrifice, than the name of a senator or of an alderman causeth them to think upon old age, or to imagine that every one so termed must needs be ancient because years were respected in the first nomination of both.
>
> Wherefore to pass by the name, let them use what dialect they will, whether we call it a Priesthood, a Presbytership, or a ministry, it skilleth not: although in truth the word *Presbyter* doth seem more

fit, and in propriety of speech more agreeable than *Priest* with the drift of the whole Gospel of Jesus Christ.[1]

False beliefs will also indirectly affect the validity of a sacrament if they lead the minister to change the rite in essentials. If, for instance, the Saracen's heathenry led him to substitute the name of Allah for the Trinitarian invocation, or if a minister's Macedonian beliefs led him to omit the name of the Holy Ghost, there would be no Baptism.

It is necessary and sufficient for validity that the form in priestly Ordination express the bestowal of the Christian priesthood (stated or understood to be a sacrificing priesthood) or of its grace and power. The Anglican form of 1552, which lasted without essential change for over 100 years, was: "Receive the Holy Ghost: whose sins thou dost forgive, they are forgiven; and whose sins thou dost retain, they are retained. And be thou a faithful Dispenser of the Word of God and of His holy Sacraments." Obviously this expresses the bestowal neither of the priesthood nor of its chief and specific power. The word "priesthood," which in a Catholic form is sufficient because in the Church's formularies it bears its true sense of sacrificing priesthood, does not occur at all in this form. Indeed, in the "traditio instrumentorum," which immediately follows the actual form, the power of sacrificing is clearly and positively excluded by the substitution of the Bible for the chalice and paten which are delivered in the Catholic rite. In view of this it can hardly be held that the phrase "Dispenser of [God's] Sacraments" "definitely signifies" the specific power of the Catholic priesthood. The phrase is far too vague. What sacraments are referred to? A layman can confer Baptism, and only a bishop can ordain, bless the chrism for Extreme Unction or (normally) confirm. What sacraments, then, are meant? Since in the sixteenth century there was a great flowering of the English genius for theological compromise, it is possible that even at the time no one could have answered this question with assurance. The sacrament of Penance cannot be excluded with complete confidence, since the 1552 Prayer Book has a ceremony which might be a sacramental absolution of a penitent (provided he be sick). A form, however, expressing the conferment of the power to forgive sins would

[1] Hooker, *op. cit.*, Book V, Chap. lxxviii; my italics in *"although ... sacrifice."*

not suffice for the bestowal of the priesthood; and in any case it seems safer to interpret "the sacraments" in this context by the English Church's official doctrine as contained in the XXXIX Articles. Since the Articles recognise only two sacraments, Baptism and the Lord's Supper, it is presumably these that are meant. Of these the former can be conferred by a layman, and the sacrificial character of the latter (as well as the Objective Presence) is denied explicitly in the Articles and implicitly in the Ordinal itself.

The word "priesthood" does occur several times in the Edwardian rite outside the essential part. But, apart from the fact that the word is absent from the form, what does "priesthood" mean here? Hooker gave a clear answer thirty years later; and, independently of that, if the Anglicans insist on the rite being judged as a whole, then, in deciding whether the Ordinal embodies the Catholic, the evangelical or some intermediate conception of the Christian ministry, due weight must be given to the substitution of the Bible for the chalice and to the deliberate omission of the repeated references to the priest's sacrificial function which were so prominent in the Sarum ritual. The Edwardian Ordinal must primarily be judged precisely as a corruption of, and in contrast with, the Catholic rite which it displaced.

2

The Argument of Gregory Dix

I

SINCE legal arguments and decisions are largely the scientific application of common sense, it should not be surprising that the validity of a sacramental form is determined in much the same way as the validity of a legal instrument transferring property or investing a person with some power or office. Just as the legal document or ceremony must definitely express the conveyancing of the property or the bestowal of the power, so it follows from the nature of a sacrament that the rite of Ordination must definitely express (by naming it, or equivalently) the Order, or its power, being bestowed and the fact of its bestowal. It was on this principle that Leo XIII declared Anglican Orders invalid, because of defect of the form: "Receive the Holy Ghost: whose sins.... And be thou a faithful Dispenser of the Word of God and of His holy Sacraments."[1] The Reformers violently mutilated the Sarum rite in order to exclude the power of offering the Body and Blood of Christ.

Time and again in *The Question of Anglican Orders* Gregory Dix with the utmost perversity interprets Leo's statement as meaning that *both* the Order and its power (of offering the Christian Sacrifice) must be expressed and, further, must be directly mentioned.[2] Since, naturally, several early Catholic Ordination rites did not explicitly mention *both* the Order of priesthood and its (inseparable) power, the natural effect of Dix's grave exaggeration of Leo's requirements is to sow confusion. For Dix thus enables himself to conclude an ostensibly serious historico-

[1] Cf. *Apostolicae curae*, Denzinger, *Enchiridion* (ed. 24-25), n. 1964; C.T.S. (H. 311) translation, n. 25.

[2] *The Question*, etc. (Dacre Press, 1944, 1945), p. 46; the assumption underlies the whole discussion on pp. 46-58.

theological inquiry into the essentials of the rite of priestly Ordination with the ludicrous statement: "One thing is clear beyond dispute. If the conditions laid down for a valid 'Form' ... in *Apostolicae curae* are indeed a necessity *sine qua non*, then there are now no valid orders anywhere in Catholic Christendom."[1] Coming on top of his carefully phrased discussion of some early rites, this preposterous assertion might conveniently leave the inexpert reader with the impression that, in the midst of such (really inessential) diversity, it is hardly possible to define an objective canon of a valid form.

II

Dix's first line of defence is a paradoxical one. Explicitly recognising the analogy of a legal document, he yet admits that the 1552 Ordinal was substantially Cranmer's work and, secondly, that "Cranmer personally was probably seriously heretical about the meaning of Ordination."[2] These are indeed important, if unavoidable, admissions: how, one wonders, is the situation to be retrieved? The trump card turns out to be (of all things) the XXXIX Articles of 1562. Before 1562, Dix argues, the English Church was not consulted; the two Ordinals and the Act of Uniformity were forced by the Government upon a powerless and reluctant Church (Thomas More, Cuthbert Mayne, Edmund Campion and many others preferred to die). The fact, therefore, that Cranmer probably "personally intended to express an heretical intention in his new Ordination rites" "has simply no bearing whatever on the theological question of Anglican Orders."[3] For as soon as the Church was free to speak, it formally repudiated Cranmerist theology—in the XXXIX Articles.

One comments, first of all, that the theological views of the compiler or compilers of the Ordinal cannot be completely ignored. For the overwhelming presumption is that they will find expression in the Ordinal; in fact Cranmer's detestation of the Mass is clearly expressed in the Ordinal—most manifestly in the compilation of a radically new form which omits all the sacrificial phrases and ceremonies of the Sarum rite which it displaced. There are limits to the extent to which an orthodox intention can be "put upon" a heretical form.

But it is the appeal in this context to the Articles which is really

[1] Dix, pp. 57–58.   [2] 33; cf. 31–35.   [3] 33; cf. 35.

astounding. "We are not 'Cranmerists' but Anglicans," Dix writes;[1] Cranmer, the argument is, denied the Mass and the Real Presence, but the XXXIX Articles teach—well, what *do* they teach? Article XXVIII ("Of the Lord's Supper") makes it perfectly clear that Christ is not, in the Communion service, either offered or really present. After stating (what is, of course, implicit in the Supper symbolism) that the Eucharist is a partaking of the Body and Blood of Christ, the Article goes on to explain how this is to be understood. "Transubstantiation," it says, ". . . cannot be proved by Holy Writ, but is repugnant to the plain words of Scripture . . . and hath given occasion to many superstitions." Before quoting the next sentence it is worth noticing that Dix, referring to it, blandly informed his layman correspondent that "for Cranmer's flat denial" of the Real Presence the Church of England substituted, in this Article, "the assertion that 'the body of Christ *is given*' in the Eucharist."[2] The Article actually reads: "The Body of Christ is given, taken, and eaten only after an heavenly and spiritual manner. And the mean whereby the Body of Christ is received and eaten in the Supper, is Faith." Compare Article XXXI which repudiates the Mass as a "blasphemous fable."

III

The "matter" in priestly Ordination is the first imposition of hands (in silence) by the bishop. The "form" is the Preface, the essential words being: "Bestow, Almighty Father . . . the dignity of the Priesthood. . . ."[3] The form, therefore, is the prayer, in express or equivalent terms, that the candidate may be (or the statement that he is being) made a priest. Absolutely speaking, an *explicit* statement that power over the Body of Christ is being conveyed is not necessary in a Catholic rite, since in a Catholic context "priest" *means* one ordained to consecrate and offer the Body of Christ and to be "steward" to Christ's Mystical Body by dispensing the sacraments.

In addition, however, to this primitive and essential rite, the Catholic ceremony, as developed by the time of the fourteenth century, contained also the anointing of the hands, the delivery of the instruments (chalice and paten), and two other impositions

---

[1] 33. [2] 34; Dix's italics. Cf. the Preface, above, pp. 9–10.
[3] Cf. Pius XII's Apostolical Constitution, *De Sacris Ordinibus*, A.A.S., 40 (1948), 5–7.

of hands, the last being accompanied by "Receive the Holy Ghost: whose sins . . ."; this last ceremony was introduced only *c.* 1200. It is not surprising that the medieval theologians, not being skilled in the methods of modern critical history, commonly held that one or more of these secondary rites were essential. St. Thomas, for instance, held that it was the delivery of the instruments which conferred the priestly character and power; and it was almost universally held from the thirteenth to the sixteenth century that the delivery of the instruments was at least one of the essentials.

But whatever medieval theory said, and it was at no time quite unanimous, they in fact never *omitted* any part of the approved rite. Even when (faced with a number of *prima facie* possible matters and forms) they erred theoretically, they were too good Catholics to discard any part of the rite which *might* be essential. Cranmer, good scholar as he was, was not good enough; in the infatuation of his heresy he abandoned both that rite in the Pontifical which was commonly held to be essential (thereby manifesting his heretical mind) and also the part which (as Dix agreed) was in fact the essential form.

Moreover, the medievals, in spite of the fun Dix pokes, were right in adopting a partly *a priori* method in their theoretical inquiries; they therefore never lost sight of the conditions a valid form must fulfil. Dix's own purely inductive method, on the other hand, yields only the ludicrous negative conclusion (based on a deplorable misreading of *Apostolicae curae*) that none of the five early rites he examines fulfils the conditions laid down by Leo.[1] His method has, however, the incidental controversial advantage of suggesting to the uninitiated reader that the whole question is wrapped in such impenetrable obscurity that, in defining the minimum requirements for validity of rite, one cannot get much beyond the formula "imposition of hands with prayer": that the *nature* of that prayer hardly matters and that it need not, as Leo required, definitely signify the bestowal of the sacrificing Christian priesthood.

IV

All the early Catholic rites examined by Dix[2] in fact clearly fulfil Leo's requirements. Four of them expressly declare that the presbyterate (priesthood) is being bestowed. The fifth, the

---

[1] Dix, 56–58.   [2] 44–58.

Serapion rite, is commonly cited by Anglicans as a difficulty for Catholic theory. But Serapion's "matter" is correct, and the "form" expresses perfectly in its own (fourth-century Egyptian) idiom the essentials of the Christian priesthood. The form is: "(A) Let Divine Spirit come to be in him (B) that he may be able to be a steward [dispenser] of Thy people and (C) an ambassador of Thy divine oracles [the Gospels], and (D) to reconcile [$καταλλάξαι$] Thy people to Thee ... (E) Who didst give of the Spirit of Moses upon the chosen ones, even Holy Spirit."[1] Here we have prayer for the bestowal of the Holy Spirit (A) and of authority to preach the Word (C). (B) may mean "a dispenser of the mysteries [sacraments] to Thy people" (cf. 1 *Cor.* 4.1). But the important phrases are (D) and (E), of both of which Dix quite misses the point. The presumption that the reference in "reconcile" is to Christ "reconciling both [Jew and Gentile] to God ... by the cross"[2] and in general to the (in scriptural language) "reconciliation" wrought on Calvary and perpetuated in the Mass, is made certain by a comparison with the same Serapion liturgy where "reconcile" ($καταλλάξαι$) occurs between the two Consecrations at Mass. There the celebrant briefly prays: "We beg of Thee, by means of this Sacrifice be reconciled ($καταλλάγηθι$) with all of us. ..."[3] This is to say, Serapion understood the "reconciling" of the Christian people to God to be principally achieved at Mass, and his Liturgy in effect defines *katallaxis* as what happens at Mass, so that the empowering of a priest to *katallaxai* means giving him power to offer Mass.

Dix's comment on (E), that "the chosen ones of Moses" "were not sacrificing priests," is true but misleading. The point is that Moses is the great type of Christ, standing in the same relation to the Old Law as Christ to the New. Moses' plenary position, therefore, typifies the High Priesthood of the New Law; and it was Moses who anointed Aaron and consecrated him High Priest.[4] Moses' assistants, therefore, the seventy "elders" (presbyters), here, as in the old Roman and early medieval Western

[1] English translation from Dix, p. 46; for the Greek text cf. Gebhardt and Harnack (ed.), *Texte der Altchristlichen Literatur*, N.F. II (Leipzig 1899), p. 11 in the Egyptian section.
[2] *Eph.* 2. 16; cf. 2. 13 and 2 *Cor.* 5. 15 and 18.
[3] Greek text in *Texte, etc., ibid.*, p. 5.
[4] *John* 1. 17: "The law was given by Moses; grace and truth came by Jesus Christ." Cf. *Matt.* 5–7 and Stephen's speech in *Acts* 7. 20–44; *Numbers* 11. 16, 24–25; *Leviticus* 8. 1–15; Cyril Hier., *Cat. Myst.* 1. 3.

rites, typify the holders of "the office of second merit" in the New Law, *i.e.*, Catholic priests.

V

Dix rejects "the old 'High Church' apologetic" which inclined to regard Cranmer and his colleagues as "premature Tractarians." He himself, while admitting that Cranmer was a Protestant of "the extreme 'left-wing' variety," urges that he "—like all the Reformers—is a product of the late medieval tradition."[1] Surely both these views are perverse and the truth is that, like the Tractarians, Cranmer wanted a return to the primitive Church, but, unlike so many of them who saw that the primitive Church was Catholic, adopted extreme Protestantism (for which he died) precisely because he thought the primitive Church was Protestant.

In a deplorably misleading page[2] Dix proceeds to suggest that in composing a new Ordinal Cranmer was motivated by a desire to get away from the medieval "tangle" and to simplify the rite. Did Dix really expect anyone but his Anglican lay correspondent to believe that this was the motive underlying the substitution of the delivery of the Bible for the delivery of the chalice and paten with the words: "Receive power to offer sacrifice to God, and to celebrate Masses for the quick and the dead"? And was it a mere coincidence that it was precisely the sacrificial phrases and ceremonies of the Pontifical which without exception were abandoned? Surely it is more natural to connect the rejection of the words just quoted with the Article (XXXI) which echoes them: "Wherefore the sacrifices of Masses, in the which it was commonly said that the Priests did offer Christ for the quick and the dead ... were blasphemous fables."

Dix then states that "a whole school of medieval theologians" had regarded the words "Receive the Holy Ghost . . ." as the essential form (as in the 1552 Ordinal). Who were these unnamed theologians, forming "a whole school," who held that this rite *alone* was the sufficient essential? If there was such a school, it formed a small and undistinguished minority.

As an example of this school Dix takes the Council of Mainz, held "not twelve months before the first *Ordinal* was compiled."[3] It is an unfortunate example. It is surprising that so eminent a scholar should not have bothered to find out the full facts. One

[1] 59; cf. 31. [2] 67. [3] 67; cf. 62–3.

thing is certain about this Council of 1549: it taught that *several* ceremonies, including the delivery of instruments as well as the imposition of hands, are indispensable parts of the essential rite. The Council states that by imposition of hands with "Receive the Holy Ghost . . ." the bishop imparts the power of the Keys. It then declares explicitly that the priest's central and essential power of sacrificing is conveyed by the delivery of the chalice and paten ("potestatem tradit offerendi Deo hostiam sanctam et placabilem").[1]

VI

Dix began by admitting that the Ordinal was composed by extreme left-wing Protestants, who imposed their liturgical forms on a helpless Church. In this first defence the situation was saved by the XXXIX Articles by which, as soon as she won her freedom, the Church "imposed" an intention on the new Ordinal. Towards the end of his book Dix seems to have seen that the Articles were a bad bet. "The authoritative interpretation" of the Ordinal is now given by its preface.[2]

The Preface expresses the intention of "continuing" the three Orders of bishops, priests and deacons, which have been "in Christ's Church . . . since the Apostles' time." Now, the intention here expressed would be perfectly satisfactory as the subjective intention of the minister. The minister need have no more than a "blind" intention of doing "what the Church does," what Christ instituted, "whatever that may be." But the subjective intention cannot heal a defective *form*, and the trouble with the Ordinal is precisely its defect of form. The Preface, therefore (being no part of the form even in the widest sense), can help only as evidence of the "intention" (meaning) of the form; and from this point of view it is only a fraction of the total evidence, and is hopelessly outweighed by the other evidence, notably the Articles and the deliberate mutilation—a mutilation which speaks for itself—of the Catholic rite. Moreover, the Preface itself is highly ambiguous. It offers no guarantee that the Catholic reality, as distinct from the names, of bishop and priest is being retained. That these new priests do not offer the sacrifice of the Mass is clear from the mutilation of the Catholic Ordination rite and from the Articles.

[1] *Constitutiones Conc. Prov. Moguntini* (1549), in the Bodleian Library copy, pp. 213–231, esp. 230.
[2] Dix, 82–3.

If further evidence is needed of the Protestant character of the Articles and the Ordinal, one has only to go to the sixteenth-century Anglican theologians. A generation or so ago Anglicans could be found willing to defend the Catholic orthodoxy of Cranmer's Eucharistic doctrine. Cranmer is now abandoned: "Cranmer himself," Dix tells us, "was probably seriously heretical about the meaning of Ordination."[1] The views of Cranmer's contemporaries, Tyndale and Hooper, were unambiguously heretical. For Tyndale a priest was simply an elder (so called "because of his age, discretion, and sadness"), and a bishop an "overseer."[2] Hooper wrote: "the office of bishops and priests in the primitive and first church was to be preachers of God's word and ministers of Christ's sacraments; not to sacrifice for dead nor live, not to sing or mass, or any such like."[3] Nowadays for evidence of the Catholic legitimacy of the Church of England we are bidden to look rather to the Elizabethan divines. But they were no less definitely heretical, as anyone can verify by taking down the admirable volumes of the Parker Society if he suspects the following necessarily brief quotations of being unrepresentative. They are primarily intended to arouse the curiosity of those Anglo-Catholics who naïvely believe that in their stand against Dr. Fisher and his allies in the dispute over South India they have the support of their Church's symbols and official formularies and of the Anglican tradition.

The extant writings of Jewel, Fulke and Hooker leave no doubt that in their views about the Eucharist and the ministry these theologians were no less definitely heretical than Cranmer, Tyndale and Hooper. "The servants," said Jewel, the accepted contemporary exponent of the new religion, "knew not who sowed the tares; neither do you know who founded your Mass." William Fulke explains that etymologically "priest" is the same word as "presbyter" and therefore "should signify naught else but an 'elder'... that is, one appointed to govern the Church of God according to His word, but not to offer sacrifice for the quick and the dead."[5] Hooker lists among the "sins of Babylon" the doctrines "that the bread in the Eucharist is transubstantiated into Christ; that it is to be adored, and to be offered up unto God, as a sacrifice

[1] p. 33.   [2] Parker Soc., II 253.   [3] P. S., I 480.
[4] P. S., III 338-9.   [5] P.S., I 242.

propitiatory for quick and dead."[1] In the light of the English Reformers' reiterated repudiation of "sacrifice for the quick and the dead" it is altogether unnecessary to guess, with Dix, at their motive in dropping, in the new Ordination rite, the delivery of the instruments with the accompanying words: "Take power to offer sacrifice to God and to celebrate Masses for the quick and the dead." The Reformers' harping on this phrase is likewise an admirable commentary on the 31st of the XXXIX Articles with its repudiation of "sacrifices of Masses... for the quick and the dead"; by comparison with it, one finds strangely unconvincing such modern commentaries as that of Bicknell who, finding great virtue in the plural nouns, states that what the Article rejected was not the Mass itself, but unsound theories of the Mass.

A study of the sixteenth-century Anglican divines, then, leaves still unanswered the question Who *are* the "Catholic" theologians among the Founding Fathers of *Ecclesia Anglicana*? It is consequently difficult to attach much importance to the Anglo-Catholic argument based on the Preface's apparent implication that men already possessing (Catholic?) Orders will be accepted for the Anglican ministry without re-Ordination. According to the XXXIX Articles, after all, Ordination was not a sacrament. Why should not ex-Catholic priests have been permitted, indeed encouraged, to abandon the Mass and to "collaborate"? It was to be expected. This arrangement, like the ambiguity of the Preface itself, simply reveals the cynicism of a Government anxious to foster the blasphemous fiction of "continuity" and to hoodwink the people of England into a betrayal of their ancient Faith. Fifteen centuries earlier Augustus had known the technique. The Senate was preserved, the shadow of a shade; nominal consuls were elected annually; no single magistracy was abolished. But the Republic had perished.

[1] *Discourse on Justification:* cf. Works, III (6th ed., Oxford 1874), 497–8.

3

The Ordinal of 1552

I

IT IS AGREED by all that the Catholic validity of Anglican Orders stands or falls with the rite of the second Ordinal (1552), which remained unchanged for over a hundred years. Since a sense of proportion is easily lost in attending to the subtle abstractions inseparable from a detailed refutation of Anglican objections, it is best to begin by stating the positive argument which shows clearly and certainly that the Catholic priesthood cannot be conferred by this rite.

While the analogy of a legal instrument brings out the point that a sacramental form must "definitely signify" the office (or its essential power or powers) being conferred, the principles by which the meaning—and hence the sufficiency or insufficiency—of a sacramental form is determined may best be seen from the analogous case of credal formulas or other theological documents.

It is a commonplace that in judging the orthodoxy of an early Christian writer who has used some vague, ambiguous, or technically incorrect expression, it makes all the difference whether he was writing before or after the relevant heresy had arisen. Several of the early Fathers, for instance, writing before the Nestorian heresy, used expressions which could easily bear a Nestorian sense; but because they wrote before the Nestorian heresy, these expressions are given the benefit of the doubt and are interpreted in an orthodox sense, even although, if written after Nestorius, they would be condemned.

Similarly one does not expect to find the word "consubstantial" in orthodox ante-Nicene theological works or in a very ancient formula like the Apostles' Creed. But if a conciliar Creed composed after Nicaea omits the word, then, however apparently

THE ORDINAL OF 1552

edifying or scriptural its language, it is at once gravely suspect. Consider, for instance, the teaching concerning the Son in the "Dated Creed," imposed by force upon a reluctant Church by Constantius II in 360: "And in one only-begotten Son of God ... begotten before all ages ... God from God, like to the Father that begat Him according to the Scriptures."[1] A reader unversed in theology might judge that this compared very favourably with the simple "and in Jesus Christ, His only Son, our Lord" of the Apostles' Creed. But, after Nicaea, the real significance of the "Dated Creed" lay in what it omitted to say; the Son was in fact being declared neither consubstantial nor even "like in substance" to the Father. Hence St. Jerome called the Creed Arian, and it is generally recognised that it was heretical and that its imposition marked the temporary defeat of orthodoxy in the East.

Similarly when one finds a new Ordinal created just at a time when there was violent controversy about the Mass and the nature of the priesthood, and when this new Ordinal, composed in defiance of the Catholic Church, omits all the sacrificial phrases and rites of the Catholic Pontifical, and when, further, the most influential theologians of the new Church as well as its official Articles rejected the ideas of Transubstantiation, Real Presence, and sacrifice—then, surely, it is a hopeless case.

There is no help, therefore in the suggestion latent in Dix and C. F. Hrauda, that, in spite of the heretical beliefs of its composers, the new rite might, by a sort of happy accident, have been patient of an orthodox interpretation. Such a thing could, indeed, have happened; the abstract possibility is clear from the fact that a high proportion of theological terms—not only faith and justification, but priest, sacraments and Eucharist—were used in common by both Catholics and Protestants, although in very different senses.

Even if, however, Cranmer had happened to compose such a superficially ambiguous form, a simple form (*e.g.*, "Vouchsafe, Almighty God, to make this man a minister of Christ's sacraments to assist the bishop") which might conceivably have served in the early Church, such a rite, when framed in the sixteenth century, could no more be valid than a fifth-century conciliar Creed containing neither the word "consubstantial" nor its

---

[1] There is an English text of this creed in *Documents of the Christian Church* (ed. H. Bettenson, Oxford University Press, 1946), pp. 61–62.

clear equivalent could be orthodox. The Anglican rite, even if it had so achieved ambiguity, would still have to be judged primarily as a deliberately mutilated rite, by clear implication denying the Mass and the Catholic conception of the priesthood.

Nor could the situation be saved by the ordaining minister's having the intention of doing *quod facit Ecclesia*, or "what Christ instituted." For, while this implicit or "blind" intention would suffice as the *subjective* intention (intention of the minister), a sufficient subjective intention cannot heal a defective form. Nor may the objective intention (the meaning of the form) be "blind"[1] in this sense; the form must definitely express the correct meaning —the effect actually intended and achieved by Christ.

II

This last principle shows the fallacy in the following passage in *In Terra Aliena*:

> Leo XIII's argument narrows down to the question of defect of intention. [After quoting St. Alphonsus the writer continues] According to St. Alphonsus, it is then possible for the minister, without imperilling validity, to reject the doctrine and practice of the Roman Church, so long as he intends to conform to that of the true Church.... The Reformers certainly did not intend to do what the Roman Church does, but can we accuse them of not intending to do what the true Church... does? Not in the face of the preface to the Anglican ordinal.... However heretical the Reformers may have been, here is a clear declaration of their intention to do what the true Church... does. In the case of earlier rites of unquestioned validity the intention was no more explicitly stated than in the Anglican form of ordination. The intention in the case of the earlier rites was secured apart from the form. The intention in the case of the Anglican ordinal also is secured apart from the form, *viz*., in the preface.[2]

There are two errors here, either of which alone would invalidate the argument. The writer supposes that according to Catholic doctrine the subjective intention can heal a defective form, and, secondly, that the meaning of the *form* can be "blind." St. Alphonsus was speaking of the subjective intention of the minister. His doctrine is that a Mohammedan can baptise validly, so long as he performs the rite properly with the intention

[1] See footnote on p. 12. [2] P. 8.

of doing what the Church does, or what the Christians do. If, however, he "rejects the *practice*" of the Roman Church, not just in the sense of regarding the whole thing as superstition, but in the sense of changing the rite, then there is no Baptism. Even an explicitly orthodox subjective intention cannot heal a radically defective form; still less could this "blind" intention which—quite rightly—is all that V. Roberts claims to find in the Anglican preface. And for Leo, of course, it was the defect of form that was primary and decisive.

In the case of the early Catholic rites the intention was *not* secured apart from the form. The form, though simple, bore the correct meaning in its Catholic context; it did not attain its shape through mutilation of the Catholic form by heretics (not that, even apart from this consideration, there is any real analogy between these early forms and the Anglican form).

V. Roberts appears to have recognised that the Preface expresses no more than the "blind" intention to create the sort of ministers which Christ instituted, "whatever that may be." He recognised that the English Reformers' conception of the priesthood was heretical. But the Preface could help the form, if at all, only by an explicitly orthodox statement of specific intention, which would be evidence of the orthodox *meaning* of the form.

III

How does one judge the sufficiency of a sacramental form? How far are the beliefs and intentions of the compiler (or compilers) of the 1552 Ordinal relevant?

If the objective meaning of the form is clearly either orthodox or heretical, one need go no further. If there is any doubt, the historical origin and context of the form are relevant in a high degree, and the character of the new rite as a whole is highly relevant to the interpretation of the form in the narrower sense. The authentic interpretation implicitly given to the Ordinal by the 25th, 28th and 31st of the XXXIX Articles is equally relevant. The omissions in the 1552 Ordinal (as compared with the Pontifical) are of the first importance. If a heretic happened to compose an unquestionably orthodox form, his personal beliefs and intention would not matter. But in practice a composer of a new form who intends to express an heretical intention is likely to succeed in producing a form with a heretical meaning. Even if he should happen to produce a *prima facie* ambiguous form, remarkable mainly for what it omitted, this form would be (like a fifth-century Creed lacking the "consubstantial") heretical.

IV

Of the two defences of Anglican Orders to which Anglo-Catholics commonly appeal, one, that by Gregory Dix, has been examined in the previous chapter. The other, a posthumous work by C. F. Hrauda entitled "Anglican Ordinations," occupies the greater part of three numbers of *Reunion* for the years 1945-46.[1]

After Hrauda's early remark that "Anglican apologists . . . mostly seem to show a weak grasp of the distinction between the personal intention of the *minister* and the intention of the *rite*,"[2] it is surprising to find the argument of this learned and scrupulously fair study vitiated at key points by this very confusion.

Quoting Bellarmine, Hrauda shows that the minister need not intend to do what the Church *intends*, but only what the Church *does*.[3] Bellarmine was speaking of the intention of the minister. Hrauda then unwarrantably introduces into the discussion of the *form* this distinction between the Church's external action (pouring water, saying "This is my Body") and her specific intention in this action—to regenerate or transubstantiate. For in discussing the question what kinds of heresy are liable to invalidate an Ordination form, he mentions only heresies concerning such (partly) external matters as the three-fold ministry, Episcopal Ordination and the Apostolic succession. Astonishingly, he says not a word in this section about heresies concerning the priesthood, transubstantiation, and sacrifice.[4]

The externalism of Hrauda's view appears most clearly where, seeking to show that the Ordinal's conception of a priest is Catholic, he writes that the Ordinal's priest "can perform the sacred action instituted by Our Lord at the Last Supper. . . . This action consists in reciting Our Lord's words [of Institution], of receiving the consecrated elements and administering them to the faithful."[5] It is quite clear from Hrauda's thesis as a whole that he did actually hold that this mechanical view of the priesthood suffices for the "intention" of an Ordination form; as if the

[1] *Reunion* (Baxter's Press, Oxford), June and December 1945, June 1946. The pages are numbered consecutively throughout.
[2] *Reunion*, p. 66.   [3] 69; cf. 70-73.
[4] 73-79.   [5] 83; cf. 84.

THE ORDINAL OF 1552

power to transubstantiate and to offer Christ slain in sacrifice were irrelevant to the Catholic conception of the priesthood! For on page 148 he actually writes: "We know that the reformers in general did not believe in the Sacrifice of the Mass in the true sense, and therefore did not intend to confer the power to sacrifice." A comparison of this page (148) with pages 67–73 shows that the origin of this astonishing doctrine is a transference to the form of teaching that applies only to subjective intention. This erroneous view is, in fact, a modified, but still fatal, version of the contention that the form, like the intention of the minister, can be "blind."

V

The form of the 1552 Ordinal immediately follows the imposition of hands and is as follows: "Receive the Holy Ghost: whose sins... And be thou a faithful dispenser of the Word of God and of His holy Sacraments."

The Holy Ghost is bestowed in Confirmation. "Whose sins..." is neither the traditional form nor the New Testament form of ordination—the Apostles were ordained at the Last Supper and were already priests when they received the power of the Keys in *John* 20. 22-23. Nor is it an apt form for ordaining priests. That is clear from the fact that the whole sentence, "Receive... are retained," was spoken by Our Lord to men who were already priests. Hrauda asserts that the formula, "Receive the Holy Ghost," "had, at the period of the Reformation, acquired the force of a conventional signification of the conferring of Holy Orders, or Major Orders."[1] But what Hrauda needed to show was that in the new Ordinal this formula signified specifically and exclusively *Catholic* Orders.

Hrauda next argues that the words, "Whose sins...," show that it is specifically the priesthood which is being conferred. It is already clear from several places in the Ordinal that what is in question is the Ordination of priests of some sort; but it is equally clear that the Ordinal did not know how to proceed in the matter.

A form which simply specifies a secondary power, one of the priest's powers in relation to Christ's Mystical Body, and says nothing about power over His physical Body, cannot confer the priesthood, even if, as Hrauda argues, this secondary power were

[1] 137.

distinctive of the priesthood. It is only on the preposterous hypothesis that in Protestant theology the absolving power *by convention symbolised* the sacrificing priesthood that this form could conceivably suffice. Since the question is one of meaning, Dr. Messenger correctly argued that the form could suffice only if the separation of the absolving from the sacrificing power were *inconceivable*. Hrauda's comment, "From the point of view of Catholic theology it *is* inconceivable," is relevant only in reminding us that the Ordinal was not inspired by Catholic theology.[1] If Protestant theologians believed at all in the power of the Keys, they believed that it was separable from the power to say Mass. Indeed, "Receive the Holy Ghost, whose sins . . . " was the form of the (non-episcopal) Ordination rite of the Hessian Reformed Church.

Hrauda's insistence that the absolving power has never *in fact* existed separately from the sacrificing power is rather like the other Anglican argument, that a Christian priest is in fact and by definition a sacrificing priest. But the Reformers did not *think* so. The Editor of the *Church Times* has frequently and emphatically asserted that "the Catholic Church in this country" means the Established Church; if he were to bequeath all his property to "the Catholic Church in England," it would be of no use His Eminence of Westminster and the English Catholic Bishops claiming the property on the ground that, as they in fact represented the only true and real Catholic Church in this country, they must be the persons signified in the will.

On page 151 Hrauda writes: "Where you have the words of institution pronounced over bread and wine by a priest, with the intention of doing what Christ instituted . . . there you have the Mass, even though neither priest nor people believe it. So . . . in the words, 'Be thou a faithful dispenser . . .,' the power to offer sacrifice is implicitly conferred." This is a perfectly circular argument: the minister ordained by the Ordinal says Mass (even though the Ordination rite has not led him to expect to do so), and he is a true priest because the meaning of the Ordination rite must be orthodox, since in fact he says Mass.[2]

There is space for only a cursory discussion of the final phrase,

---

[1] Cf. E. C. Messenger, *The Reformation, the Mass and the Priesthood*, Longmans, Green and Co., II (1937), 700; Hrauda, 139-40.

[2] The same circular argument appears on p. 146.

"And be thou a faithful dispenser. . . ." Since the Eucharist is sacrament as well as sacrifice, it is not surprising that similar descriptions of the priest's functions are occasionally found when these are very briefly summarised in Catholic sources. Yet Hrauda very fairly accepts Messenger's statement: "The phrase ('the ministry of the Word and the Sacraments') was in current use among the English and Continental Reformers, and was employed by them specifically to distinguish the functions of the ministry as these Protestants conceived it from the sacrificial function of the Catholic priesthood."[1] After that he can only argue that the English Reformers showed their independence of certain of their Continental brethren by retaining such externals as the Apostolic succession, and that "God's sacraments" are *in fact* the sacraments as Catholics understand them—an argument vitiated by the "ontological fallacy" examined above; here again, the question is one of meaning.

The salient facts relevant to a true judgment of the 1552 Ordinal are these. The Ordinal was a violent mutilation of the Catholic Pontifical; it omitted the sacrificial phrases of the Pontifical; it omitted the anointing of the hands which should handle the Body of Christ; it substituted for the delivery of the chalice and paten the delivery of the Bible; it was composed by heretics at a time when heresies about the Mass were raging, yet contains nothing approaching what alone in such circumstances could save it—an unambiguous bestowal of power to sacrifice; the XXXIX Articles confirm its heretical character.

[1] Hrauda, 142; Messenger, II, 704. More precisely, Hrauda admits this explicitly of certain Continental Reformers, and does not deny it of the English Reformers.

PART II

4

Dr. Mascall on Ordination

I. OCEANIA

IN HIS PAMPHLET,[1] as in his long letter to the *Church Times* of 28 October 1955, Dr. E. L. Mascall persists in assuming, against the plain meaning of the text, that the principal defect which Pope Leo XIII, in his *Apostolicae curae*, found in the second Edwardian Ordinal was a defect of intention. It was in fact a defect of form. Dr. Mascall's mistake is excusable insofar as this confusion of minister's intention and the meaning of the form of the sacrament has bedevilled discussion ever since the Anglican Archbishops, referring to a passage in *Apostolicae curae* in which Leo referred to intention in the traditional sense, used the phrase "the intention of the Church" in a sentence which was relevant only if interpreted as designating the *meaning put upon the form by* the officially expressed doctrine and intention of the Church using the form.[2] It is, indeed, a consolation to

---

[1] *The Convocations and South India*, Mowbray, 1955.
[2] There can be no two views about where Leo placed the emphasis, namely, on defect of form; one has only to read chaps. 23–33 of the Bull to see that. This certain fact is independent of the question whether in chap. 33, where Leo imputes defect of intention, he is speaking of subjective or objective intention. It seems in fact clear that "intention" in this chapter (quoted in full in Appendix II below) means subjective or ministerial intention. For (1) this is the traditional meaning of the word in sacramental theology. (2) The defect found by Leo is presented as distinct from, though connected with, defect of form. (3) It is inferred from defect of rite and of objective intention (the meaning of the form). (4) The whole argument of the chapter proceeds on the explicit assumption that the intention in question cannot be directly known, but can be judged only in so far as it is externally manifested—by the retention of the Catholic rite or, contrariwise, the introduction and use of a novel, heretical rite. (5) Thus the third and fourth sentences speak explicitly of the minister and give the traditional criterion of validity of ministerial intention. The Holy Office applied the same principle (with the opposite result) in the Oceania case where, the rite having been kept, sufficient ministerial intention was presumed. (6) Nowhere in the

lesser men to find a giant like Dr. Mascall, some of whose contributions to theological studies have been so valuable, guilty of this unfortunate confusion. The consequences, nevertheless, are deplorable.

Dr. Mascall writes in his pamphlet: "It is not always realised what very slight intention is required . . . for the valid performance of a sacrament."[1] We, at least, realise it clearly; we have long been familiar with the teaching of Bellarmine and Sylvius on the point. Dr. Mascall continues, astonishingly: "The minimising nature of the traditional Western doctrine of intention is sometimes obscured by the fact that Roman Catholic controversialists in England have found themselves in the uncomfortable position of having to defend the condemnation of Anglican Orders by Pope Leo XIII and of having to improvise special theories and distinctions in the attempt to maintain the defective intention [sic] of Anglican ordinations without at the same time rendering the orders of the Roman Church itself of doubtful authenticity." Let us repeat: all this rests upon a deplorable confusion. The gravamen of the charge against the Ordinal of 1552 is that the *form* had not the Catholic *meaning*; it did not, as a sacramental form must do, "signify the grace" of the sacrament. The rite introduced by the Reformers in place of the Catholic Pontifical did not signify the priest's essential supernatural power to consecrate and offer the Body of Christ. By

chapter does Leo speak of the effect or grace of the sacrament, or of the intention of the Church or of Christ (expressed in the form) but of the existence (*ut sit*) and nature of the sacrament, of Christ's institution, and of what the Church *does*. (7) So far from supporting the other view, the "therefore" and "connected (*coniunctus*)" in the first sentence confirm this view. For "therefore (*igitur*)" introduces, strictly, not a summing-up but an inference. And, while defect of objective intention, being virtually the same thing as defect of form, cannot strictly be connected with or inferred from it, defect of subjective intention is a corollary of defect of form due to deliberation. (See also Appendix I below.)

In their *Reply* to *Apostolicae curae* in 1897 (reprinted by S.P.C.K. in *Anglican Orders*, 1954: cf. pp. 31-32, 48-49) the Anglican Archbishops, referring to this chapter, understood Leo as meaning "the *intention* of a Church," and themselves used this latter phrase in the sense of the meaning put upon a form by a Church's official formularies, a sense which approaches that of objective intention. The Archbishops, of course, being unfamiliar with the technicalities of Catholic sacramental theology, were hardly to blame for this misconception of a chapter which has sometimes been interpreted by Catholics as referring to objective intention. What has been so unfortunate has been the consequent confusion of ministerial intention and the meaning of the form, and the tendency of Anglicans to judge the second by a criterion applicable only to the first.

[1] P. 9. All references to the pamphlet are to pp. 9-12.

commission and omission it signified the denial of the essential priestly power. Leo was thus basing himself on the first principle of sacramental theology, namely, that sacraments, being symbols, "must both signify the grace which they cause, and cause the grace which they signify,"[1] and he judged the Ordinal of 1552 invalid on the ground that, introduced at a time and in a place where heresies about the Mass and the ministry were rife, it removed from the Sarum rite every reference, in action, prayer or phrase, to the priest's power to transubstantiate and to offer. It was the origin, character and spirit of the Ordinal itself which, above all, Leo examined and judged unsatisfactory. It is true that he then added one brief paragraph about intention, the paragraph (33) beginning: "Cum hoc igitur intimo formae defectu coniunctus est defectus intentionis"; but the main weight of his indictment fell on the rite itself, and his secondary charge of defect of intention was an inference from the Reformers' change of the rite. There is, therefore, no truth in the accusation that the Oceania case shows that Catholics have devised special theories or distinctions to defend the condemnation of the Edwardian Ordinal. The Oceania baptisms were valid because the form was kept, and Anglican orders are invalid because the form was changed.

For intention it suffices that a person performs the rite seriously, as a sacrament. Thus a young priest rehearsing the ceremonies of the Mass, or "practising" baptism, neither consecrates nor baptises, because he does not intend to say Mass or baptise. In the other sort of relevant case, a Buddhist can baptise if he intends not just to bath the baby, but to do what the Christians do. A heretic or pagan, that is, can confer the sacrament of baptism (and does if he intends to) even though he disapproves of it, disbelieves its efficacy, or has erroneous opinions about its effects.

If, however, the false beliefs of a Church lead it to change the form of the sacrament, or (as they so easily can in Orders) result in the very word "priest," "presbyter," or "bishop" having an un-Catholic *meaning*, then, of course, the sacrament is invalid. Both hypotheses are relevant to the second Edwardian Ordinal and (particularly the second) to ordinations in CSI, whose *Constitution* states that the acceptance of episcopacy "does not

---

[1] *Apos. curae*, C.T.S. (H 311) trans., chap. 24; Denzinger, *Enchir. Symb.* (1928, ed. 16, 17) n. 1963.

commit it to any particular interpretation of episcopacy *or to any particular view or belief concerning orders of the ministry.*"

Dr. Mascall, however, still pursuing the wrong hare, both in his pamphlet and in his letter introduces the case of the Methodist Oceanian baptisms into his discussion of Anglican and CSI Orders. But the Methodist baptisms in Oceania have nothing to do with either case, since in these there was no question of defect of form (the rite being properly performed), but alleged defect of intention. The Central Oceania case was this. When some natives who had been baptised by Methodists (who do not believe that baptism regenerates) later became Catholics, the Consultors of the Holy Office declared in 1872 that although it was "openly preached in the sect," and sometimes explicitly declared by the minister before he baptised, that baptism "had no effect on the soul," these facts did not justify them in automatically declaring the baptisms in all cases doubtful because of defect of intention in such sort that they should all be conditionally repeated. The Consultors saw that the Oceania case was simply the old case of baptism by a Saracen over again. In the consideration of the Saracen type of case it was naturally assumed by the theologians that if the Saracen had been asked before he baptised whether he believed that baptism had any effect on the soul, he would have replied in the negative. But neither Saracen nor Methodist is necessarily prevented by his false *belief* about the *effects* of the sacrament from *intending* to confer the sacrament. The whole point of a sacrament is that *when it is properly* (form) *and seriously* (intention) *performed*, it works automatically, *ex opere operato*.[1]

Dr. Mascall errs in saying that the Holy Office declared the baptisms valid. The point of the Holy Office's reply was that neither in Saracen nor Methodist baptism do false beliefs ground a certain and final presumption of defect of intention. As they obviously do not. The reply of the Holy Office meant, not that all the Oceania baptisms could be considered valid without further inquiry, but rather that they should not all be repeated without further inquiry. Thus the Holy Office stated in a *coda* elucidating its reply that the intellectual errors mentioned "cannot

---

[1] Proper dispositions in the adult recipient are required for the sanctifying grace proper to the sacrament, but not for receiving the character or power bestowed by such sacraments as baptism and holy orders.

in themselves create such a general presumption against validity ... as of itself to justify a practical principle of universal application in virtue of which *a priori* [*i.e.*, without further inquiry into what the ministers of the sacrament did in fact *intend*] the baptisms should be repeated."[1] Beliefs and errors belong to the intellect, intention to the will. Surely a Saracen, much more a Methodist, can pour the water intending to perform a Christian rite? Only on the extremely improbable supposition that the frame of mind of the Methodists in question was such that if they had somehow learnt the truth about the sacrament, they would have refused to proceed, would the baptisms have been invalid. But evidence suggesting such an intention would have had to be elicited by inquiry into *intention*; it cannot be settled by evidence about beliefs.

Neither, of course, do false beliefs about the nature of the ministry and the Eucharist ground a presumption of defect of intention to bestow the sacrament of Order. But what they very easily do is to invalidate the *form* of the sacrament by essentially changing its meaning. The Catholic Church could validly use the form, "I make you a presbyter"; in the Church's use of the word "presbyter" would be a transliteration of the Latin word, and so would mean a priest. But used in a Church which chose the word "presbyter" in preference to "priest" precisely to signify the evangelical conception of the ministry, the form would be invalid.

But may not false beliefs about baptism also, then, change the meaning of the word "baptise?" No: while Murray's *New English Dictionary* cites plenty of evidence of the two radically different meanings of "priest," and quotes J. B. Lightfoot as noting that "the word 'priest' has two senses," the word "baptise" has only one meaning in a Christian context: "to apply water as a sign of Christian initiation." Moreover, while the laying on of hands is indeterminate in its symbolism, in baptism the washing symbolises the cleansing from sin (and so, indirectly, regeneration) and the naming indicates the birth of the "new man." Moreover, by no principle of semantics could the rite of baptism (instituted directly by Christ Himself, who also gave it its meaning) be construed as bearing the *opposite* of its true significance. Finally, there is always an extremely strong presumption in favour of the

[1] *Collectanea*, S.C.P.F., 1465, *anno* 1877.

validity of a sacrament in the performance of which the minister has observed with exact fidelity the rite prescribed by Christ and hallowed by the Church's usage.

II. Identifiability

In his letter, Dr. Mascall proposes the novel doctrine that in sacraments whose forms were not directly instituted by Our Lord, "identifiability" (as this or that sacrament) provides a criterion of the validity of the form. To know whether a rite is valid, he holds, it is sufficient that it be clear whether or not someone is being baptised or ordained or absolved. Dr. Mascall is satisfied if the rite "makes it clear what is being done; for example, that a bishop is being consecrated, and not a baby being baptised or a helicopter being dedicated." It is immediately obvious, first, that this criterion is extremely vague and, secondly, that it begs or by-passes all the relevant questions.

Dr. Mascall's own interpretation of his principle as applied to the sacrament of Order turns out to be mechanical and external. For him, a rite purporting to be an ordination rite is valid if it is "identifiable" as the bestowal of "a specified one of the three orders of the historic ministry"—however the order or the historic ministry is conceived. "A rite," he insists, "is a means of doing something, not a theological statement of the nature of what is being done"; and he is emphatic that in Orders the meaning officially attached to the words priest or bishop (why not elder and overseer?) by the Church using the rite is completely irrelevant.

Dr. Mascall observes that "*in the strict sense* it is only the minister who . . . can have an intention. The rite . . . cannot intend anything; it is not alive." It is true, and it has been emphasised in previous chapters that a rite *has* not an intention. "The intention of the rite" is Anglican terminology. The point is that a rite has a *meaning*—indeed, its power to symbolise or signify is its very essence—and this meaning may be orthodox or unorthodox. Ordination rites may signify either the supernatural powers of the Catholic priest or merely the evangelical conception of the ministry. A rite, says Dr. Mascall again, can "make it clear what is being done." Exactly; either alone or as interpreted by the formularies of the Church using it, the rite can make it clear whether a man is being ordained a Catholic priest or an evangelical minister. What has confused the issue about CSI orders is that the case against their validity has usually been stated in terms of the ambiguous or misleading Anglican phrase, "the intention of the Church." Like the case against the Edwardian Ordinal, the case against CSI orders is (setting aside the question of the quality of the ordainer) based on defect of form. An interpretively evangelical ordination form is an implicit denial—and a denial not just in intention but in the very form—of the sacrificial functions of the priest. Dr. Mascall says that a rite "is not a theological statement"; it is not, of course, a statement of any kind; it is a rite, a religious symbolic rite; but it implies theological statements, and signifies realities describable only in theological statements.

Disallowing any reference to the formularies of particular Churches—formularies which in fact interpret their ordination forms—Dr. Mascall further urges that in actual fact there is really only the one Church. There is clearly a very important sense in which this is true. But it is not the one Church that determines the meaning of the word "presbyter" in the other Churches; and the all-importance of the (publicly) recognised meaning of a sacramental form derives from the very nature of a sacrament. If a Church whose presbyters are acknowledged elders ordains a presbyter, it ordains, or appoints, an elder. If it were otherwise, the form, "I make you an elder," being the true equivalent of the *ex hypothesi* valid form, would itself be valid. There is no magic in the words priest and bishop when, by the rejection of the Christian Sacrifice, they are voided of their significance. If two provinces of the Church decided to break away, reform themselves, and have elders and overseers instead of priests and bishops, but one of the two happened to keep the old names, ordinations would be equally invalid in both.

The question under discussion is this: how is the validity of a sacrament decided when the form is not (as in baptism it is) fixed, or specifically instituted, directly by Christ? In these cases the form is settled by the Church. To decide the question of the validity of forms departing from the Church's form, there are two criteria. If the rite as a whole (that is, matter and form together) signifies the grace of the sacrament, it is valid. Secondly, if the new form is an accurate paraphrase or equivalent of the

Catholic form, it is, again, valid. For most theologians would agree that while it is sinful to depart from the regular form without grave reason, an extemporised form with substantially the same meaning would be valid. If a priest lost his *Rituale* in the desert, he could give Extreme Unction validly by anointing the senses of the dying person to the accompaniment of extemporised prayers whose essential meaning was equivalent to that of the regular form.

How does Dr. Mascall's criterion ("is the rite identifiable as this or that sacrament?") acquit itself in problems concerning sacraments other than orders? Let us take the following pair of cases, in which there would be agreement about the solutions, and ask how the solutions are in fact reached. It will be seen that the Catholic criteria are not only relevant, but lead to reasonable solutions, while Dr. Mascall's external and mechanical criterion though it happens to fit one of the cases, is positively misleading about the other.

If a priest, instead of using the prescribed form, were to say, "As Christ's minister and representative, I forgive you your sins," it would be a valid absolution on Catholic principles. It would also be valid according to Dr. Mascall's criterion—at least if the scene were enacted in a confessional box. Suppose, on the other hand, that a Catholic priest, having lapsed into Protestantism, "absolves" a penitent by the words: "I assure you that your sins are forgiven in virtue of your saving faith." On Catholic principles this form would certainly be invalid; it is not an act of pardon; it is not, indeed, the bestowal of anything; it is simply the expression of an opinion. Dr. Mascall would presumably agree that the form is invalid. But he does not know this by his principle of identifiability (identifiability cannot be a *criterion*); and by the sort of external standards he applies to orders, the sacrament would appear to qualify for validity. The scene presents, after all, a confessional box, a clergyman in surplice, a violet stole, and a devout confession of sins; and even the unsatisfactory form itself is much more like a sacramental absolution than a harvest festival or a motor-bus.

It will be noticed that, although a sacramental form is not, strictly, a "theological statement," the differences between valid and invalid forms are both semantic and theological differences, and this fact confirms the view that relevant analogies to sacramental forms are presented by legal forms, or instruments, and Creeds. Moreover, Dr. Mascall himself makes some theological assumptions. He presumably demands at least that three historic orders be recognised, though Dr. Jalland recognises only two, and that the presbyter be conceived as exclusively entitled to celebrate the Eucharist. But why precisely these requirements, neither less nor more? Surely the questions of the nature of the Eucharist and the essential priestly power are much more important matters?

It is pretty clear how Dr. Mascall's surprising doctrine came to seem plausible even to himself. Still confusing form and intention, he thinks his principle deducible from the Roman decision about the Methodist baptisms in Oceania. He writes: "What the 1872 decision implies is that, once the *identity*[1] of the sacrament is clear, then no error about the nature of the rite . . . can impair its validity." Whether this sentence is in itself true or not depends on just what is meant. But what is obvious and important is that no inferences whatever about a criterion of validity of *form* can possibly be drawn from the Oceania case, since that case concerned intention and started from the assumption that the form had been rigidly adhered to. Yet Dr. Mascall, confusing the two, proceeds to apply to form the quite different and infinitely slighter requirements really sufficient (as the Oceania case shows) for intention. For what the Oceania case really shows, of course, is that, if the form is kept, intellectual errors do not ground a final presumption of invalidity of intention.

Since the principle of "identifiability" begs all the relevant questions, it is useless as a criterion. Asked how to distinguish between valid and invalid rites, how to recognise a true ordination rite, Dr. Mascall answers in effect: "It is recognised by its recognisability; an ordination rite is identified by its identifiability as an ordination rite." An ecclesiastical student accompanies him to an ordination in South India and, as they view the rite together, asks: "Is this a valid ordination rite?" "Yes, certainly," Dr. Mascall will reply, "if it is clear that the men are being ordained." Yet the questions are many. One asks whether, so far as their forms go, an ordination rite is valid in CSI? in the Methodist Episcopalian Church? in the Swedish Lutheran Church? when

[1] My italics here, as also in quotations on pp. 43-44.

it uses the word "priest"? "presbyter"? "elder"? "overseer"? when it does not signify the supernatural and invisible powers of the priesthood (which for nearly 2,000 years the sacrament has been understood not only to bestow, but to signify)? when it implicitly excludes these? when there is no physical contact at the laying on of hands? In these and a hundred other cases one can determine whether the ceremony in question is identifiable as an ordination rite only if one knows *beforehand* what are the requirements for a valid form. The Red Queen stamped her foot. "Go into the wood," she said, "and bring me back a Hobbit, or—off with your head!" "But, please, your Majesty, I don't know what a Hobbit is," said Alice timidly. "Then first of all," said the Queen, "you must *identify* it." "But I haven't done Identification yet," said Alice, thinking it was Quadratic Equations. "Why, look for its distinguishing marks, silly!" said the Red Queen more kindly, catching the Dormouse a smart crack with her flamingo. "Is it clearly marked, then?" asked Alice, her spirits rising again. "Very plainly indeed," said the Queen, spreading her fan: "it is marked exactly like a Hobbit."[1]

[1] Chap. 4, above, differs slightly from the December article by way of addition (I have expanded the second footnote) and, in two places, subtraction. These changes do not affect any questions, whether of fact or principle, at issue between Dr. Mascall and myself.

5

The Hunting of the Hobbit

A Reply

By

E. L. MASCALL

I HOPE I shall not appear to be merely making a debating point if I begin my reply to Fr. Stephenson's courteous and learned article[1] by remarking that perhaps the chief handicap with which an Anglican is faced in discussing the Roman Catholic case against Anglican orders arises from the fact that he can never be quite sure what that case is going to be. Fr. Stephenson says that I am mistaken in supposing that it is defect of intention that is in question in the present controversies about orders in the Church of England and the Church of South India: "in both, what is in question is defect of rite, particularly of the form." Nevertheless, he himself admits that the question of intention cannot be ignored; it hardly could be in view of the words which he quotes from *Apostolicae curae:* "*Cum hoc igitur intimo formae defectu conjunctus est defectus intentionis.*" Nor am I sure that all Roman Catholic theologians are as confident as he is that the question of intention is secondary. Quite recently I met the argument that the Anglican ordinals of 1550 and 1552 were perfectly sufficient, but that the willingness of the Anglican bishops at the time to use so novel a rite must be taken as evidence of a deliberate intention to exclude from the ordinations in which they used it the effect which in her ordinations the Catholic Church intends. Again, in a letter in *Theology* of November 1936, Fr. Henry St. John, O.P., introduced a distinction between internal and external intention and then argued that, while only the barest minimum of *internal* intention is needed for validity (so that the well-known statements of Bellarmine, Adrian

[1] *The Month*, December 1955.

Fortescue and others could be accepted), Anglican orders were nevertheless invalid through a defect of *external* intention, manifested by the use of a new "form or matter." That Fr. St. John's "defect of external intention" is not quite the same as Fr. Stephenson's "defect of rite" is shown by his statement that "a *person making use* of such a new form or matter does not therefore *intend* to do what the Church does" and his reference to the Reformers' "externally manifested intention in compiling *and using* the new Ordinals" (italics mine). I think, therefore, that the question of intention is still worth discussing.

It is perhaps well to remember that Bellarmine in a well-known passage (*De Sacr. in gen.*, I, 21) lays it down that the mere introduction of a new rite does not invalidate a sacrament, even if the new rite is introduced in the erroneous belief that the Church in which the old rite was used was a false Church and not the true one, so long as it is intended to do what the true Church does, whatever that may be, and not to introduce a completely novel rite which the true Church (whatever that may be) has never known at all. This is, of course, not conclusive in the present case, for Fr. Stephenson's case against the Anglican rite is not merely that it was novel, but that it was intrinsically insufficient; nevertheless, as the main evidence of its insufficiency is alleged to be its novelty, the point made by Bellarmine is worth bearing in mind. Incidentally, it should be remembered that the form or matter used in the reformed ordinals was "new" only in a relative sense. Some of the medievals held that the imposition of hands was the matter and some that "*Accipe Spiritum Sanctum* . . ." was the form; Rome itself did not settle the question until 1947, and then with the express provision that no judgement was being made upon the past.

As regards the Methodists in Oceania in 1872 (and one wonders what those innocent natives would have thought if they had known in what context they would be discussed in 1955!), Fr. Bévenot, S.J., has been kind enough to point out in *The Tablet* of 12 November, 1955 that I was departing from accustomed usage in describing the explicit declaration of those who baptised them (namely that "baptism had no effect upon the soul") as manifesting an explicit intention to exclude the effects which the Catholic Church believes baptism to have. He remarks that what was wrong with these missionaries was a mistake of belief, not a misdirected intention, and I think he is strictly correct. You cannot, in the strict sense, explicitly intend to exclude an effect unless you believe that the effect would occur if you did not intend to exclude it. If this is so, then the Anglican Reformers certainly cannot be accused of a defect of intention. For nobody has ever accused them of believing that ordination normally conferred sacrificing priesthood, while explicitly intending that their own ordinations should not confer it; the accusation has always been that they did not believe that sacrificial priesthood could be conferred by any ordination whatever. They had, in fact, a mistake of belief, not a misdirected intention. Even this is largely inferential. Many of the Reformers were prepared to admit sacrificial priesthood, if only it was carefully defined; and the need for such definition is clear when one considers some of the views about priesthood and sacrifice which were current at the end of the Middle Ages. We have had to wait for the present century for writers like de la Taille, Vonier and Masure to do something to restore the balance. Practically all that Fr. Stephenson has to say about Oceania I gladly accept. As he says, "only on the extremely improbable supposition that the frame of mind of the Methodists in question was such that if they had somehow learnt the truth about the sacrament, they would have refused to proceed, would the baptisms have been invalid." I submit that we must also say that, only if the frame of mind of the Anglican Reformers was such that if they had somehow learnt the truth about sacrificial priesthood (assuming that they did not know it already) they would have refused to proceed, would their ordinations have been invalid—invalid through lack of intention, that is; defect of rite is another matter, which we must go on to consider. The only point about intention that remains obscure is what precisely was the defect of intention which, even if it was secondary to defect of form, Pope Leo XIII claimed to have discovered in Anglican orders; Fr. St. John had quite a clear view about this, but all that Fr. Stephenson tells us is that Pope Leo's "secondary charge of defect of intention was an inference from the Reformers' change of the rite."

To pass, then, from Oceania to Identifiability, and Fr. Stephenson's charge of defect of rite. In the case of the Methodist baptisms, he rightly observes, there was no abandonment of the traditional and dominical form, while in the case of the Anglican ordinations there was substituted for the old rite a new one which, in his opinion, "was certainly invalid, because it was a departure from the accepted and long-established Catholic form in most significant circumstances, and the heretical beliefs of the Reformers (unlike those of the Methodist ministers) found expression in a new rite." In view of the fact that nobody knows who, with the probable exception of Cranmer, the compilers of the Anglican ordinal were, this statement seems rather sweeping. I should prefer to emphasise the words of Pope Pius XII in his Apostolic Constitution of 30 November, 1947, where he says, with reference to the *porrectio instrumentorum*, "If the will and precept of the Church have, for a time, made it necessary to the very validity of ordinations, yet it is still known to all that the Church can change and abrogate what she has established";[1] though I should want to add that the question must not be begged by assuming that the Church, in this context, must mean the Roman See. What is equally to the point is that Fr. Stephenson seems to have fallen into a confusion in his use of the words "rite" and "form." Referring to "forms departing from the Church's form" (itself a question-begging phrase if applied to the Anglican ordinals), he writes: "If the rite as a whole (that is, matter and form together) signifies the grace of the sacrament, it is valid." Now the matter and form of the priesthood, as defined by the Pope in 1947, certainly make no reference to "the grace of the sacrament," namely the power to offer sacrifice and the like; there is merely a general reference to "the dignity of the priesthood" and "the second hierarchical degree"; so if Fr. Stephenson really means by "rite" simply form and matter he cannot claim the support of the Pope. Elsewhere, however, he sees validity as determined by something very much more than mere form and matter. He would undoubtedly agree that a particular form (such as the Anglican form of 1662) might be valid or invalid according to the circumstances of its use.

Now it is obvious that words mean nothing if they are deprived of all context; I agree with Fr. Stephenson here. And I agree that we must consider the "rite as a whole" in deciding validity, if only for the reason that nobody is still quite sure just what, in Roman ordinations performed before 1947, the form and matter of orders were, and because, as I have just remarked, it seems

[1] Trans. C. Journet, *The Church of the Word Incarnate*, I, p. 118.

difficult to identify rite simply with form and matter. I suppose we must take "the rite as a whole" as meaning the complete ordination service, in its context in the life of the Church. But what precisely are we to understand by "signifying the grace of the sacrament"? Does this require an explicit statement of the whole theology of the sacrament? Clearly not, for that would be physically impossible. Does it require, then, a statement of the essence of the character bestowed by the sacrament, and if so how comprehensive and how explicit must such a statement be? This is a matter about which theologians may well differ, and indeed do differ in the Roman Church. Is it, for example, impossible to know whether a rite which "departs from the Church's form" confers the episcopal character until Roman Catholic theologians are agreed whether the order of the episcopate is essentially different from that of the presbyterate or not? This hardly seems likely. Again, in the case of ordination to the presbyterate, can it really be necessary for validity that the rite should explicitly refer to the power to offer sacrifice, at a time when that power had not been clearly defined and was often understood in an erroneous and superstitious way? (I have in mind for example the "insane" opinion for which Melchior Cano rebukes the future Cardinal-designate Ambrosius Catharinus that "sins committed before baptism are remitted through the Sacrifice of the Cross, but all post-baptismal sins through the Sacrifice of the Altar.") I do not think I am setting up such an "external and mechanical criterion" as Fr. Stephenson suggests when I assert that what is necessary for a valid rite is that it shall be possible to identify what is being done but that it is not necessary for the rite to give a theological statement of its effect. Any other criterion will lead to endless questions as to whether the theological statement is adequate to "signify the grace of the sacrament" according to the theological fashions of the day. And it is important to recognise that there *are* theological fashions, even in the Roman Church, as we see, for example, if we compare the Eucharistic theology of Catharinus, Cano, de Lugo, de la Taille and Masure. This fact raises extremely difficult questions for theologians of any communion about the relation between the unchanging content of the revelation committed by Christ to the Church and the varying modes in which the Church in its practical exposition and its theological formulation expresses that content at different times. I have no easy answer to this problem, which seems to me to be one of the basic outstanding problems of theology, but my complaint against Fr. Stephenson is that he hardly seems to recognise its existence. He does, however, touch upon the main point with which we are concerned here when he remarks, that, in the case of the authorised rite of the Catholic Church, no question about the adequacy of the form arises; everybody can identify the act which is being performed and no questions need be asked. That is why nobody ought to make embarrassing enquiries as to how the form of ordination in the Roman pontifical (as that form was defined in 1947) "signifies the grace of the sacrament." The same is true when the form is dominically instituted, as in baptism. It is, in fact, not at all easy in this last case to see that the form does "signify" the grace that the Church believes it to bestow, namely the abolition of the guilt of original and actual sin, regeneration and incorporation into Christ; were that so, the Methodists in Oceania could hardly have used it believing as they did.

Here, however, I must rebut Fr. Stephenson's accusation that in laying down identifiability as a criterion of validity I have fallen into the fallacy of arguing in a circle; this is where we hunt the Hobbit. According to Fr. Stephenson, when asked how to distinguish between valid and invalid rites, how to recognise a true ordination rite, I answer in effect: "It is recognised by its recognisability; an ordination rite is identified by its identifiability as an ordination rite." I neither said nor implied anything of the sort. What I said was that a valid ordination rite could be recognised by its declared purpose of conferring one of the three orders of the historic ministry. If, on the other hand, a rite declared its purpose to be the conferring of a new kind of ministry which had never before existed in the Church, it would be identifiable as an ordination rite and as an invalid one. Nevertheless, I think there is a point at issue between us, and that it is a very important point indeed. When the preface to the Anglican ordinal declared that its purpose was the continuation of the threefold ministry which had existed "from the Apostles' time," it was pointing to a concrete recognisable entity, and there were very solid reasons for doing this. In the first place, at a time when the essential nature of the priestly character was still not conclusively defined and when many of the concepts of sacrificial priesthood which were prevalent were such as Roman Catholic theologians themselves would later come to agree in rejecting as erroneous and superstitious, there was a lot to be said for avoiding theoretical statements which might well turn out to need revision and for pointing instead to the concrete reality which it was intended to perpetuate. Secondly, while not in the least denying that ordination confers an objective character (as the Anglican Archbishops themselves insisted in their reply to Pope Leo XIII), I would maintain that the *primary* effect of ordination to the priesthood is not the investing of an individual with priesthood as a *quality* but his incorporation into the Priesthood as an *organic entity*. To overlook this is to treat priesthood as a logical universal rather than as a flesh-and-blood reality in the world of space and time, to make concessions to the individualistic outlook which has marred so much medieval and post-medieval theology, and to detach the individual priest with his priestly character from the Church as a concrete and organic whole; its natural culmination is the recent massive work of Mgr. Journet, who bases his ecclesiology not upon the doctrine of the Church as the Body of Christ but upon the hierarchy as (in the Aristotelian sense) the Church's efficient cause. Priesthood, I would affirm, is not simply or primarily a logical universal particularised in a number of individuals, but a concrete reality in the order of history, rooted in Christ the ascended High Priest and persisting in the world until the end of time as we know it. To the question "What does ordination effect?" the fundamental answer is given not in terms of an abstract statement (however accurate such a statement might be) but of the ministry as a historic organ of the historic Church; not in fact by talking about priesthood but by pointing to priests. There is nothing circular in this; in terms of Fr. Stephenson's parable, it is not like defining a Hobbit as a being which has Hobbit-like markings, but like defining it by telling you where it is and inviting you to go and look at it. Fr. Stephenson has characterised my criterion as external and mechanical; I might characterise his as abstract and individualistic.

I suspect, however, that at this point Fr. Stephenson and I differ on a fundamental issue, which it is difficult to settle by argument. To demand that a rite shall "signify the grace of the sacrament," in the sense in which Fr. Stephenson understands that phrase (I do not deny that it has another sense which is fully acceptable), seems to me to involve an acceptance of late medieval and Tridentine theology as normative and indeed irreformable which I cannot make. The Church of England declares its intent that the orders of bishops, priests and deacons which have been in the Church "from the Apostles' time" shall be "continued and reverently used and esteemed." The Church of South India declares that it "accepts and will maintain the historic episcopate" and that "continuity with the historic episcopate will be effectively maintained." Both of them go into a good deal of detail about what bishops, presbyters and deacons are and do. I believe that the Church of South India is in many ways a gravely defective body, and Fr. Stephenson believes the same about the Church of England. But I do not see how on any sound principle the validity of the orders of either can be denied. I regret most profoundly—as anyone must who has the unity of Christendom at heart—that Roman Catholic theologians cannot admit the validity of Anglican orders, but my loyalty to the Church of England is strengthened by the fact that they are not altogether agreed as to why they reject it.

6

In Full Cry

A Rejoinder to Dr. Mascall

DR. MASCALL'S ZEST and skill undoubtedly add to the excitement and heighten the sporting interest of the chase. He would, indeed, be a formidable antagonist if only he had a better case. A poor case, however, is often better served by a bad advocate; clearmindedness generally serves, directly or indirectly, the cause of truth. I venture, in fact, to suggest that a re-reading of my December article shows it to be not even dented by Dr. Mascall's reply. He has largely, indeed, evacuated the main Anglican positions, recognising their indefensibility, and fallen back upon a novel, and still more untenable, line of defence. For he has virtually (in spite of some half-hearted gestures) abandoned the Anglo-Catholic attempt to show that the 1552 Ordinal somehow signified the priest's essential, supernatural powers, and now defends the astonishing position that the grace of the sacrament need *neither* be signified in the rite *nor* consciously intended (not that the latter would alone suffice). This is the principal point, on which the reader should keep his eye throughout.

But first Dr. Mascall complains that the case against Anglican orders is presented somewhat differently by different people, and, in particular, that I have emphasised the argument from defective intention less than some theologians. This complaint provides the occasion for four comments, some of which lead to the heart of the matter. First, it is the case against Anglican orders as it has been presented in *The Month* of July, August, September and, particularly, December 1955 that Dr. Mascall has accepted an invitation to answer, and he will himself, as a philosopher, be the first to acknowledge that if one argument proves a thesis, that thesis must be true; the support of the thesis between their respective requirements could be bridged, Dr. Mascall's contention would seem less revolutionary. Let us examine the arguments adduced in support of this surprising contention. Dr. Mascall argues, first, that the fact that the Oceania Methodists could baptise without believing in the supernatural effect of the sacrament is evidence that in baptism the rite does not symbolise its effect. But in December I showed in some detail how the baptismal rite does plainly symbolise or signify the effects of the sacrament. The Methodists really prove the rule in so far as they commonly believe that, though baptism does not actually regenerate, it symbolises a regeneration that has already taken place. It is not, that is, the symbolic character of the baptismal rite that the Methodists are blind to, but its efficaciousness. Secondly, Dr. Mascall is quite mistaken in saying that the matter and form of the priesthood as defined in 1947 "certainly make no reference to 'the grace of the sacrament.'" In a Catholic context the very word "priest" suffices to signify the sacrificial power; moreover the immediate context, the whole rite, whose importance Dr. Mascall recognises, expresses most vividly (*e.g.*, in the handing of the chalice and paten and the anointing of the hands, not to speak of the words, which are still more explicit) the priest's essential powers and functions. The reason why there was controversy between Catholics about which parts of the ceremony were the "matter and form" was that in the course of centuries a duplication of the essentials had occurred owing to an early amalgamation of different rites, so that the essentials of the priesthood are clearly signified in *several* parts of the developed Latin rite.

The question at issue is whether sacramental rites in general (the application of the principle to matrimony is rather obscure, but love is mysterious) signify—really though symbolically express—their grace, or whether they are purely arbitrary signs, in the minimal sense of marks, like a stone marking the place of a buried treasure. It must be remembered that there *is* a conventional element, particularly in the symbolism of the "matter"; water, for instance, could symbolise several things besides cleansing; but the accompanying *words*, the form, generally make the symbolism unambiguous and explicit. Anyone can decide for himself the truth of the matter by examining the rites of the various sacraments. Leo was justified in saying that "everyone knows" that sacraments "should signify the grace which they cause." The doctrine, indeed, is implied by ordinary language when we speak of "a sacramental view of nature," meaning that nature really shows forth invisible realities. Dr. Mascall's assertion that the doctrine is of late medieval and Tridentine origin is surely rather sweeping (if he will allow this retort, not, in intention, discourteous). The doctrine goes back to the golden age of theology and is frequently asserted or assumed by St. Thomas. St. Thomas begins by defining sacraments as signs, and he means by a sign something like a picture, something which signifies or "means" as words do, only less clearly. He explains that the reason *why* a substantial change in the form invalidates a sacrament is because the words produce their effect *quantum ad sensum quem faciunt*. He is clear that the baptismal washing really symbolises the cleansing of the soul by the infusion of sanctifying grace, and even quotes Scripture for it (*abluti estis, sanctificati estis*). He even has the doctrine that the matter and form make up the sign, the form making the meaning more precise.

As a generalisation, of course, the doctrine cannot go back beyond the twelfth century, since the seven sacraments were only classified under one category by Peter Lombard. But in reference to particular sacraments the doctrine is found in the Fathers. It would be a mistake to think that St. Thomas drew his theology entirely from Aristotle. St. Augustine defines a sacrament as *visibile verbum* and says that the water in baptism "touches the body, but cleanses the heart."

No, of course the rite need not give an exhaustive statement of the theology of the sacrament. The puzzles Dr. Mascall invents are artificial. I showed above (p. 47) that this Catholic doctrine, traditional since St. Thomas, best solves problems about validity of form (some border-line cases there must be) and that Dr. Mascall's novel criterion is useless. I dealt above (pp. 28–29) with the unfounded assertion that any medieval school of any importance held that "*Accipe Spiritum Sanctum . . .*" *alone* was the form in ordination. Dr. Mascall's problem about the episcopate was anticipated and answered by Leo XIII (C. T. S., ch. 29).

I welcome Dr. Mascall's distinction between "the unchanging content of revelation" and the varying modes of its theological formulation (though in the Catholic Church "theological fashions" are not so revolutionary as elsewhere). The distinction provides the answer to the untenable view that at the Reformation the theology of the Mass was so confused that it was impossible or undesirable either to affirm or deny the sacrificial character of the Eucharist. Questions, indeed, about the precise relation between the Mass, Calvary and the Last Supper are among the harder questions of theology, and some medieval theories were unsatisfactory. No doubt many people could not have explained lucidly just *how* the Mass was a sacrifice; but *that* the Mass was a sacrifice, in some sense Calvary re-presented, was a point of faith which it was heresy to deny. It is really absurd to suggest that there was not a straightforward conflict between English Catholics and Reformers on the central dogma; moreover, there was no suggestion of unsatisfactory theology or superstition in the ordination rite which the Reformers rejected. It was a straight question of whether a priest is or is not ordained "to consecrate and offer" the Body of Christ. And does Dr. Mascall seriously expect us to believe that the Catholic laymen who harboured priests when the penalty was death did not sufficiently know what the Mass was?

III

Briefly to hunt the Hobbit: I can only repeat that since, in this context, a criterion is that by which a thing is recognised or identified, identifiability cannot be a criterion, for that would mean that a thing was identified, and identifiable, by its identifiability. The criterion of identity, is, of course, a thing's distinguishing characteristics. Dr. Mascall's apparent adherence to his strange criterion seems to be a part of his puzzling campaign to set up an antithesis between essences and existents, qualities and the real or concrete: to suggest that existents or "organic entities" are characterless and indescribable. But qualities are as real, exist as truly, as "concrete entities." Every existent (including organisms) is characterised and consequently describable. Yet Dr. Mascall says that he cannot define the priesthood; he can only tell us where it is, or point to priests. This is very mysterious. And how can he point at it, or know where it is, unless he knows what it "looks like"? It is obvious that Dr. Mascall's *real* criterion is, after all, a set of characters. "The historic ministry," indeed, is a blanket description of the ministry; it is, however, in Dr. Mascall's use of it, an essentially defective description. It covers some external features of the ministry: the ministry must be threefold; the presbyter must have the prerogative of celebrating the Lord's Supper and the bishop that of ordaining. But the criterion omits the essential characters, the priest's supernatural powers of transubstantiating, etc.—powers without which ordination and the Eucharist lose their meaning.

But even supposing that the candidate succeeded in locating and identifying a bishop without knowing what a bishop was, Dr. Mascall's actual theory of ordination presents a number of grave difficulties. The essential priestly powers, he holds, need *neither* be signified in the rite *nor* consciously intended. All this is surely very odd—and novel. It appears to be Dr. Mascall himself who finds himself "in the uncomfortable position of having to improvise special theories." All that is required, on this view, is some form or gesture of election or incorporation into the "organic entity"—a mere invitation to accept membership would do, or the declared purpose of "conferring one of the three, etc." Again, if the inner meaning of the order conferred is irrelevant to validity, why would not the form "I make you an elder" or "overseer" serve as well as "I make you a priest (presbyter)" or "bishop"? The former pair of words are possible, indeed literal, translations of the original Greek words, and, moreover, represent the Episcopalian Methodist conception of the ministry. It is only their *meaning* (which Dr. Mascall scorns) that distinguishes them from "priest" and "bishop." Again, why, on this theory, could one not confirm validly by simply declaring one's purpose to confer the historic sacrament of confirmation, and that even though one had no idea what the true grace of the sacrament was? Again, when Dr. Mascall says that the primary effect of ordination is not the investing with the priestly character or quality, but incorporation, by "primary" does he mean logically prior or more important? If the former, then a man would be a priest logically prior to having the priestly character or quality; if the second, what is greater than the priestly character, which I suppose to be participation in Christ's eternal Priesthood? Again, while it is easy to see how the character is indelible if it is conferred immediately by the sacrament, if, on the other hand, it results from membership of an organism (presumably *qua* sacred) it is not clear why it would not be lost by sin, or at least by expulsion or excommunication. And I must here repel the charge that the ordinary Catholic view (that the rite signifies the effect and confers the character directly) is "individualistic" (and it is particularly hard to be accused of being abstract and individualistic at the same time!). Characters or qualities are the very basis of the community of things; it is in their qualities that individual existents may resemble one another. Emphasis, therefore, on the priestly character so far from encouraging an individualistic view, provides a more intelligible basis than Dr. Mascall's theory for the priestly fellowship. Finally, the most obvious objection to this original and ingenious but unsound defence is that, while on the traditional view neither heresy nor schism need in itself invalidate orders, on Dr. Mascall's view of ordination as incorporation into an organic entity (collegiate existent? concrete universal?) anything like schism must be fatal. Entry into a corporation must depend on the *will* of the corporation. Irregular admission or initiation by a few dissidents will be worthless. On this view, therefore, uncanonical or illegitimate orders must be null, as they were often regarded in the early Greek Church. The juridical aspect becomes much more important and a merely material Apostolic succession such as the Anglican, will not be enough.

Dr. Mascall, I think, ceases to be dispassionate when he studies the theology of the late middle ages and the sixteenth century (though ecclesiastical morals and discipline were corrupt enough). I long for the unity of Christendom as deeply as he does; but I see no way to it save by undoing the ill done, by unweaving the ill-woven web back to the point of tragic disaster.[1]

[1] This chapter is shorter than the corresponding article in *The Month* (February 1956) owing to the fact that prior to the decision to add the two February articles (Chapters 5 and 6) to this book, I had used my February discussion of Intention as the basis of the first two pages of Appendix I (below) on Ministerial Intention. Although in my (new) Note 2 (pp. 40–41 above) I return finally to my earlier view (*The Month*, December 1955) that "intention" in *Apos. curae* 33 must mean ministerial intention, and I no longer allow (as in February 1956) for the possibility that Leo may have meant objective intention, this does not affect my position vis-à-vis Dr. Mascall; for obviously, if Leo *had* meant objective intention, this, being practically equivalent to the meaning of the form, would provide no, even *prima facie*, basis for Dr. Mascall's contention that the principal defect which Leo found in the Edwardian Ordinal was a defect of intention, as distinct from form. See my note 2, *The Month*, February 1956, p. 97. As I there wrote: "But there can be no two views about where Leo put the emphasis. . . . It is perfectly clear, however, independently of these minutiae of interpretation, where the emphasis of the Bull falls—on the form. . . . Similarly, while I have been unable to read the *Theology* controversy, I have just had the happiness of meeting Fr. Henry St. John, O.P., personally, and, as expected, I learn from him that there is no significant difference between my view and his form-intention view in *Theology*." Certainly our discussion revealed a complete identity of view.

APPENDIX I

MINISTERIAL INTENTION

IN defining the intention requisite in the minister the Councils of Florence and Trent, using a phrase already known to St. Thomas, said that the minister must intend "to do what the Church does." St. Robert Bellarmine (*De Sac. in genere*, I, 27) explains—indeed, it seems to be common doctrine—that in this formula the words "what the Church does" denote *non finem, sed actionem*: i.e. they refer, not to the grace conferred by the sacrament, but to the rite itself (words and actions); the minister, that is, need not intend to bestow the Holy Ghost, to regenerate etc.; what he must (at the least) intend is to pour the water, to anoint etc. *as a Christian rite*—to baptise the baby, not just to bath it. The requirement may be otherwise expressed by saying that the minister must intend not just to perform a natural action, but to operate on the sacramental plane, or to perform a religious rite, or to act as the minister of Christ or of the Church.

While it is most important to distinguish between ministerial intention and form (the requirements for each being so different, since the one may be "blind" and the other not) it would nevertheless be a mistake to regard form and intention as altogether contrasted and separate. Indeed, the reason why the effect of the sacrament need not be consciously or explicitly intended by the minister is precisely because it is expressed by the rite. Moreover, the rite expresses an *intention* (Christ's or the Church's) in the sense in which (to take a legal analogy) a will both has a meaning and expresses an intention, and legal disputation about the meaning of the will is at the same time disputation about the intention of the testator. Further, the minister himself, even if his opinions about the effect of the sacrament are wildly erroneous, yet, provided always that he keeps the Church's rite, somehow intends the effect of the sacrament in so far as he intends the rite which in fact signifies the effect.

Whenever, therefore, a sacramental rite is seriously performed, form and intention, though distinct, are hardly separable. When the form is kept, subjective (ministerial) intention is presumed (at least failing decisive evidence to the contrary). Objective intention is clearly inseparable from the form, since it is simply the meaning of the form. A substantial change of the form, on the other hand, must (it would appear), even if done in good faith, destroy even the subjective intention, in so far as intention is really a modality of the rite and the requirement really is a single thing, that the minister shall (e.g.) pour the water seriously and as a sacred rite, or that, in performing the Church's action, he shall act as the minister of Christ. For the requirement about intention is really that the minister shall act ministerially, as the agent of Christ. Now, if an agent or envoy departs, even though inspired by the best of intentions, from his principal's commission, he no longer acts as an envoy. Thus viewed, subjective intention no more than objective can be had apart from the form; and even if it can be maintained that there is some sense in which a person in good faith and owing only to error blunders grossly in the rite, intends to do what Christ instituted, it is not the right sense. He might like to act as Christ's agent, but he does not do so. In any case, it is clear that form or rite is primary, and that even if a sufficient subjective intention were possible apart from the Church's form or its equivalent, it could not save a defective form.

These considerations show the significance of the fact that a Saracen who duly baptises does somehow intend the effect of the sacrament, and they show incidentally that the principles governing questions of sacramental validity are not irrational or arbitrarily legalistic, but intelligible in a broadly human way. This theoretical exploration also explains why it is so easy to read into chap. 33 of *Ap. curae* (to amplify rather than qualify the exegesis of that chapter given in note 2 above, p. 40) a meaning that transcends the narrowly technical considerations by which problems of intention are decided in practice. While the chapter applies the technical principles with precision, its (inevitable) connection of the question of intention with the question of rite inevitably points to wider and deeper considerations and reminds us that the Ordinal before the Pope is one in which the "prayers have been stripped of everything which in the Catholic rite clearly sets forth the dignity and functions of the priesthood," in the whole of which "there is no clear mention of . . . the power to consecrate and offer sacrifice" and in which, even in those prayers which were in part retained from the Catholic rite, "every trace of these things was deliberately removed and struck out" (*Ap. c.* 27, 30).

I emphasise that this Appendix in no way seeks to enlarge the requirements for ministerial intention. That a minister who performs the proper rite does somehow—perhaps quite unconsciously and only implicitly in so far as he thereby acts as a minister—intend the *effect* of the sacrament, is a descriptive, not prescriptive rule. The effect is properly considered in relation to the form. And it remains absolutely true that, in deciding sufficiency of ministerial intention, one need ask only: "Did he intend to do what the Church does?" and this question need refer only to the Church's rite. But unless a satisfactory rite is presupposed, questions about ministerial intention are hardly worth asking.

It is clear how vague and potentially misleading is the criterion of validity given by Bishop John Wordsworth, a criterion so highly regarded in the Anglican Church that it is quoted as authoritative not only by Dr. Mascall in his pamphlet but also by the United Report of the Convocations (1955) on The Church of South India. Bishop Wordsworth wrote: "The 'Sacrament of Order' requires laying-on of hands, with prayer suitable to the office conferred, and with a general intention of making a man what the Church intends as a Bishop, Priest, or Deacon." The formula will serve if "prayer suitable etc." is duly emphasised and properly explained as meaning that the form must express, either explicitly or at least implicitly (by convention and from its Catholic context) the essential priestly powers. But if the possibly blind "general intention etc." is matched by an equally blind form in a Church which does not know, or positively misconceives, the primary priestly functions, then the ordination will be invalid— owing to defect of form; particularly is this so when, as with the Ordinal of 1552, we are compelled to judge a form precisely as a deliberate departure from the Church's form.

Chap. 33 of *Ap. curae*, therefore, reinforces from another angle the point to which Leo attached such importance (chaps. 27–32), that an Ordination form cannot be judged altogether *in abstracto* and without reference to its historical context and the circumstances of its origin, and, in particular, that the Ordinal of 1552 cannot be judged as if no heresy about the Eucharist and the priesthood had ever arisen, or as we might judge an early Catholic rite, but must be judged as a departure from, and mutilation of, the Catholic rite. In this chapter 33 Leo points out that, similarly, a minister who uses a rite which departs in essentials from the rite of the Church cannot intend the Church's rite: must be presumed, that is, not to intend to "do what the Church does." (Cf. St Thomas, *S. Th.* III, 60, 7, *ad 3um*.)

APPENDIX II

The Text of "Apostolicae curae," Chap. 33.[1]

[The C.T.S. (H. 311) translation by Canon G. D. Smith, slightly adapted.]

CONNECTED, therefore, with this inward defect of form is a defect of intention, equally necessary for the existence of a sacrament. Concerning the mind or intention in itself, which is something internal, the Church does not pass judgement; but she is bound to judge of it so far as it is externally manifested. Now, if a person has seriously and duly used the proper matter and form for performing or administering a sacrament, he is by that very fact presumed to have intended to do what the Church does. This principle is the basis of the doctrine that a sacrament is truly a sacrament even if it is conferred through the ministry of a heretic or unbaptised person, provided the Catholic rite is used. But if, on the contrary, the rite is changed with the manifest purpose of introducing another rite which is not accepted by the Church, and of repudiating that which the Church does and that which by Christ's institution belongs to the nature of the sacrament, then it is obvious, not only that the intention necessary for a sacrament is absent, but also that an intention is present which is contrary and opposed to it.

[1] This Chapter 33 of *Apostolicae curae* is discussed in note 2 on pp. 40–41, and is referred to on pp. 18, 40, 42, 50, 59, 67 and 68.

APPENDIX III

A LETTER FROM WALTON HANNAH

DEAR SIR,

Fr. Anthony Stephenson's article on the theology of orders[1] is from the Anglican standpoint even more timely than he perhaps realises. For the Convocations of Canterbury and York are to be asked, not indeed at this stage to approve a full intercommunion between the Church of England and the Church of South India, but to recognise the full validity of South Indian orders insofar as they are episcopally conferred. Even among Anglicans who resist full intercommunion there seems to be little theological awareness of the implications of this step, even though such a recognition would in fact amount to a vindication by the Church of England of the bull *Apostolicae curae*, and a repudiation of the letter *Saepius officio* which the Archbishops of Canterbury and York wrote as their official reply to Leo XIII in 1897.

"In speaking of the necessary intention," writes Fr. Stephenson, "a distinction is sometimes drawn between subjective intention (the intention of the minister) and objective intention which is virtually the same thing as the meaning of the form." This distinction of necessity receives a far greater emphasis in Anglican circles, because we Anglicans fully realise that Barlow, Scory, Coverdale and a host of other consecrating bishops since may have had heretical views on the gift conferred in holy orders, and on the sacraments generally. Therefore we cheerfully endorse such statements as Fr. Stephenson's that "per se ... very little is required on the score of (subjective) intention," and that the consecrating bishop "is disqualified, so far as validity goes, neither by heresy nor schism (material or formal) nor even by apostasy." The strength of the Anglican case has always rested on the belief that the defective subjective intentions of individual consecrating or ordaining bishops are over-ridden by the objective or formal intention of the Church, particularly in our case as expressed by the ordinal in the light of its Preface.

"Nor do we part company with the Pope," wrote the two Archbishops in 1897, "when he suggests that it is right to investigate the intention of a Church in conferring Holy Orders insofar as it is

---

[1] The reference is to Fr. Stephenson's first article only (see above, pp. 15-22). Mr. Hannah's letter, though it appears here in the form of an appendix, originally appeared in *The Month* of August 1955, being occasioned by the article in the July number.

manifested externally. For whereas it is scarcely possible for any man to arrive at a knowledge of the inner mind of a Priest, so it cannot be right to make the validity of a Sacrament depend on it; the will of the Church can both be ascertained more easily, and ought also to be true and sufficient. . . . But the intention of the Church must be ascertained insofar as it is manifested externally; that is to say, from its public formularies and definite pronouncements which directly touch the main point of the question."[1]

The Archbishops of course went on to urge that the Preface to the ordinal does provide just such a public statement of adequate objective or formal intention, and with that assurance we Anglicans have, perhaps too complacently, remained content.

But after the recognition of South Indian orders such assurances can carry no further weight. The South Indian ordinal indeed is valid as regards matter (the laying on of hands with prayer) and specifies the offices of bishop, presbyter and deacon. The form is no more or less ambiguous than the Anglican ordinal of 1662, which it approximates fairly closely. But the Preface to the ordinal to which we Anglicans have pinned our faith for so long is entirely missing.

If we follow the advice of the Archbishops in 1897 and seek the intention of the Church of South India "from its public formularies and definite pronouncements," what do we find? The only public formulary of binding authority, apart from the ordinal itself, is the Constitutions of that Church, which includes its doctrinal statement.[2] And here the intention, or lack of it, is explicit and unambiguous. The ministry is referred to as the "historic episcopate," but never as apostolic or of divine foundation. "As episcopacy has been accepted in the Church from early times," it declares, "it may in this sense fitly be called historic. . . . Any additional interpretations, though held by individuals, are not binding on the Church of South India." The acceptance of episcopacy therefore "does not commit it to any particular interpretation of episcopacy *or to any particular view or belief concerning orders of the ministry.*" Even more specifically it is stated that "in making this provision for episcopal ordination and consecration, the Church of South India *declares that it is its intention and determination in this manner to secure the unification of its ministry, but that this does not involve any judgment upon the validity or regularity of any other form of the ministry*, and the fact that other Churches do not follow the rule of episcopal ordination will not in itself preclude it from having relations of communion and fellowship with them." (Italics mine.)

[1] *Anglican Orders: The Bull of His Holiness Leo XIII and the Answer of the Archbishops of England.* S.P.C.K., 1943, pp. 31-2.
[2] *The Constitution of the Church of South India*, Christian Literature Society for India, 1952. The following quotations are from pp. 9-11 and 76-7.

Here then is an authoritative statement that the objective intention of the Church of South India amounts to no more than expediency in uniting the Anglican with the nonconformist form of ministries, not the continuation of the ministry as Anglo-Catholics understand it. The practice of South India is in accordance with this pronouncement, for she is in full intercommunion with her parent nonconformist bodies in England, and their non-episcopal ministers when visiting South India may celebrate at her altars on terms of perfect equality. Therefore episcopal ordination conveys nothing essential that non-episcopal ministers have not already got.

The motive of expediency is reiterated several times in the *Constitution*. Again it says: "Some regard episcopacy merely as a form of Church government which has persisted in the Church through the centuries and may as such be called historic, and which at the present time is expedient for the Church in South India. Others believe that episcopacy is of divine appointment, and that episcopal ordination is an essential guarantee of the sacraments of the Church. Some again hold various views intermediate between these two. The acceptance of episcopacy by the uniting Churches in which there are such differing views and beliefs concerning it and concerning orders of the ministry, is not to be taken as committing the united Church to the acceptance of any particular interpretation of episcopacy, and no such particular interpretation shall be demanded from any minister or member of the united Church . . . any additional interpretations, though held by individuals, are not binding on the united Church."

This is indeed very different from the wording of the Preface to the Anglican ordinal. Yet it gives *de jure* recognition in South India to what is *de facto* the position in the Church of England.

In defence of South Indian orders from the Anglican standpoint it can only be urged that they derive without lineal breach from Anglican orders, and that it is unlikely that the subjective intention of ex-Anglican consecrating bishops after the schism of the South Indian dioceses would be different from their former intention as Anglican bishops. But this is trying to have it both ways. In England we have long urged that the objective intention of the Church overrides subjective private intention. In South India we can only hope that the subjective intention of the bishops may over-ride the declared and explicit absence of valid objective or formal intention in public statements which our previous Archbishops, agreeing with Leo XIII, bade us to rely on.

By recognising South Indian orders as fully equivalent to our own, and ours as fully equivalent to theirs, we Anglicans today who heretofore have had no doubts must surely admit that our own future episcopal consecrations are of dubious validity. For we are, in effect, admitting that the Preface to the ordinal does not really matter, does not mean what we have always taken it to mean, and might just as well never have been written. Which of course is what Rome has been saying all along.

The same varieties of interpretation of episcopacy exist in practice in the Church of England as in South India, but we Anglo-Catholics have so far maintained that ours is the only correct one guaranteed by the formularies of the Church. Once we have recognised South Indian orders, carrying no such guarantees, as fully equivalent to our own, this position simply falls to the ground. And the South Indian reunion has been declared the pattern for future reunion on similar lines at home with the nonconformists. At the 1948 Lambeth Conference the Bishops of the entire Anglican communion endorsed the statement that "We feel that in a sense our brethren in South India are making this experiment on behalf of the whole body of the Anglican Churches. They are our pioneers in this direction of the movement for unity."[1] Subsequent developments in relationships with Sweden and Scotland and in North India and elsewhere seem to be proving this prophecy correct.

The Anglican religious orders, including that of Gregory Dix, realised the danger from South India when they threatened, in 1943, to secede. Has this been forgotten? Fr. Stephenson, I suppose, would maintain that South India represents the true position of *Ecclesia Anglicana* as it has always been since Elizabethan times. If the Convocations recognise South Indian orders they will in effect be admitting that he is right.

This crisis should make us all the more grateful to Fr. Stephenson for his painstaking and scholarly analysis of previous defences of Anglican orders. If those of South India are recognised, I do not see how we can ever defend them again. But are we Anglicans logical enough to face the inevitable alternative, with all the personal sacrifices that it would lay upon us? This is a matter for prayer—on both sides—rather than for further controversy.

Yours faithfully,
WALTON HANNAH

4th July, 1955
117, Queen's Gate, S.W.7.

P.S.—Since writing this letter, both the Upper and Lower Houses of the Canterbury and York Convocations have fully recognised the validity of South Indian Orders at their sessions of 5th July.

[1] *Lambeth Conference*, 1948. S.P.C.K., Part II, p. 43.

APPENDIX IV

A Convert Explains

On 11 november, 1841, John Henry Newman made his famous protest over the Jerusalem bishopric:

Whereas the Church of England has a claim on the allegiance of Catholic believers only on the ground of her own claim to be considered a branch of the Catholic Church:

And whereas the recognition of heresy, indirect as well as direct, goes far to destroy such claim in the case of any religious body advancing it:

And whereas to admit maintainers of heresy to communion without formal renunciation of their errors, goes far towards recognising the same:

And whereas Lutheranism and Calvinism are heresies, repugnant to Scripture, springing up three centuries since, and anathematised by East as well as by West:

And whereas it is reported that the Most Reverend Primate and other Right Reverend Rulers of our Church have consecrated a Bishop with a view to exercising spiritual jurisdiction over Protestant, that is, Lutheran and Calvinist, congregations in the East ... dispensing at the same time, not in particular cases and accidentally, but as if on principle and universally, with any abjuration of error on the part of such congregations, and without any reconciliation to the Church on the part of the presiding Bishop; thereby giving some sort of formal recognition to the doctrines which such congregations maintain:

And whereas the dioceses in England are connected together by so close an intercommunion that what is done by authority in one, immediately affects the rest:

On these grounds, I in my place, being a priest of the English Church and Vicar of St. Mary the Virgin's, Oxford, by way of relieving my conscience, do hereby solemnly protest against the measure aforesaid, and disown it, as removing our Church from her present ground and tending to her disorganisation.

In his *Apologia*, Newman added the comment: "As to the project of a Jerusalem bishopric, I never heard of any good or harm it has ever done, except what it has done for me; which many think a great misfortune and I one of the greatest of mercies. It brought me on to the beginning of the end."

I have quoted this because, *mutatis mutandis*, it could stand as the statement of all those Anglican clergy who, like myself, have been and will be forced by the Convocations' decree recognising the validity of the Orders of the "Church of South India" to follow Newman. The Jerusalem bishopric was, in itself, almost irrelevant; it was a flash of light revealing the essential Protestantism of the Church of England. The bishopric lasted only for the lifetime of three bishops and is now forgotten. The "Church of South India" has the same irrelevance, the same potentialities of enlightenment and about the same expectation of life.

Those of us who had to take the Jerusalem bishopric affair into account when discussing Anglican Orders could dismiss it as a deplorable by-product of State policy imposed on an Erastian Church and, consequently, as not really touching Catholic Order. As we had swallowed Henry VIII and Cranmer, there was really no point in straining at Queen Victoria and Howley. But the "Church of South India" cannot be thus dismissed. Here there is no question of State intervention or the unfortunate necessities of the Establishment. The terms are strictly ecclesiastical and theological. All the Bishops of the Church of England, sitting officially in the Upper Houses of the Convocations of Canterbury and York, have with no dissentient voice enacted that the Orders of the "Church of South India" are as valid as their own. That is to say, *for the first time in history*, the Anglican episcopate has of its own volition defined what it means by Holy Order.

And what exactly does it mean? The "Church of South India," an amalgam of Anglicans and Dissenters, officially excludes:

(*a*) unequivocal adherence to Christian doctrine by the pronouncement, with regard to the Creeds, that it "does not intend to demand the assent of individuals to every word and phrase in them." On this point, the C.S.I. has also officially stated that "as this note formed part of the Basis of Union ... no alteration is now possible."

(*b*) belief in Catholic sacramental doctrine, by insisting that C.S.I. remains in perpetuity in communion with Nonconformist bodies whose *raison d'être* is a denial of Catholic sacramental doctrine. This denial is reinforced by the fact that in a considerable number of C.S.I. churches, wine is not used at Holy Communion (presumably as a concession to teetotallers) so that, by defect of matter, there can be no valid Communion in any case.

(*c*) belief in Catholic Orders, since C.S.I. is not only not committed to "any particular view or belief concerning Orders" but in its *Constitutions* it insists that it rules out "the acceptance of any particular interpretation of episcopacy" and enacts that "no such particular interpretation shall be demanded from any minister or member."

What possible theory of Orders, in the Catholic sense, can apply to such a body, denying the full Christian faith, denying the sacraments, denying the priesthood and denying the Apostolic Ministry? It is a *reductio ad absurdum* without parallel in Christian history that a "Bishop" who is officially not allowed to believe that he is a bishop should ordain a "Presbyter" who is officially not allowed to believe that he is a priest to administer a "sacrament" which he is officially not allowed to believe is a sacrament in the One Holy Catholic Apostolic Church in which he *is* officially allowed *not* to believe.

Yet the Anglican Episcopate has said not only that it *has* bestowed valid orders on this body, but also that those C.S.I. orders are now equivalent to its own. By so doing, it has explained the meaning it attaches to the Ordinal of the Book of Common Prayer and so defined the intention of the Anglican ordination rite in an indubitably heretical sense.

Until 5 July, 1955, I, in common with every other Anglo-Catholic priest, was content to rest on the argument that the Preface to the Ordinal of 1552—the low-water ebb of Protestantism—could be (because there was no expressed intention otherwise) interpreted in the Catholic sense. It allowed us to hold—so we said—that if St. Peter was a sacrificing priest, the late Bishop Barnes, whatever his private views, was a sacrificing priest.

That argument is now impossible, for, on 5 July, 1955, the whole Anglican episcopate officially attached to the rite a specific meaning which destroys every vestige of orthodox intention.

For myself, preaching on 6 July, I said that "yesterday the Church of England, as we have known it, came to an end." Since that day the body which still calls itself the Church of England is, in fact, only the English branch of the undenominational "Church of South India," and in leaving it I cannot feel that I am deserting the body in which I was ordained priest twelve years ago in the belief that it was "a branch of the Catholic Church." There is no such body left to desert. And with gratitude for the light I see at last that the One Holy Catholic and Apostolic Church into which I, in common with all Christians, was baptised and in which I have, in the Creed, regularly professed my belief is what St. John Fisher called "Christ's Catholic known church," the Church of Rome.

HUGH ROSS WILLIAMSON